Exporting: Key Considerations for International Business Growth

Exporting: Key Considerations For International Business Growth

Products, Communication, Brands, Trade Shows, Channels, Culture, and Cash

Laurent Houlier and John Blaskey

BEP
BUSINESS EXPERT PRESS
Leader in applied, concise business books

Exporting: Key Considerations For International Business Growth—Products, Communication, Brands, Trade Shows, Channels, Culture, and Cash

Copyright © Business Expert Press, LLC, 2020.

Cover image licensed by Laurent Houlier, 2018

Cover and interior design by Exeter Premedia Services Private Ltd., Chennai, India

First published in 2020 by
Business Expert Press, LLC
222 East 46th Street, New York, NY 10017
www.businessexpertpress.com

ISBN-13: 978-1-95253-844-5 (paperback)
ISBN-13: 978-1-95253-845-2 (e-book)

Business Expert Press International Business Collection

Collection ISSN: 1948-2752 (print)
Collection ISSN: 1948-2760 (electronic)

First edition: 2020

10 9 8 7 6 5 4 3 2 1

Printed in the United States of America.

Abstract

Globalization or international development is more vital than ever for a business to survive, let alone grow. This book equips the reader to take advantage of genuine export opportunities.

The book addresses the fears and risks associated with exporting and reassures the reader that international growth is available to any business that conducts in-depth research, adopts the right attitude, and develops a comprehensive strategy.

Readers will be challenged to resolve seven of the key business considerations facing them when seeking success in export markets: product and service adaptation, comprehensive communication, portable protected branding, high-performance tradeshows, optimized go-to-market channels, fit-for-purpose internal organization, and controlled effective cashflow.

This concise book serves time-starved small to medium enterprise (SME) entrepreneurs, owners, and directors in any industry (products and services) aiming for international or global development. It is designed for businesses anywhere in the world. This book is also directed toward those studying or teaching international business.

The authors have a track record in designing and executing successful export strategies, and they share their personal experience. It is designed to take the reader beyond current books which typically cover transactional aspects, for example, export documentation, tariffs and duty, and so on. This publication draws on real commercial examples and their outcomes and focuses on the bigger picture, what is really at stake, balanced with what is realistically achievable.

Keywords

Global development; sustainable; risk mitigation; multichannel distribution; omnichannel expansion and globalization; worldwide website, e-commerce, e-marketplace, Internet; business-to-business (B2B); direct-to-consumer (D2C); intellectual property, trademarks, patents, Web domain registration and protection; compliance, packaging, labeling; pricing; translation, humor; credit insurance, currencies, payment terms, cashflow, incoterms, VAT, custom duty and clearance, tariff; distributor, agent, licensing, franchising, consignment, sale or return, concession, outlet, store, retail, subsidiary, merger, acquisition, joint venture; traffic, literature, presentation; international payment transactions; returns policy.

Exporting: "to send goods to another country for sale"
Cambridge Dictionary

Exporting: "to market goods or services beyond your home territory, and your comfort zone, to grow your business and your people."
Houlier and Blaskey

Contents

Acknowledgments

Writing this publication was inspired by a highly respected business guru who believes everyone has a book in them.

The very fact that an authentic Frenchman and a true Brit have partnered in an *entente cordiale*, despite writing at the time of Brexit, is in itself a miracle. And, we are still speaking to each other. In English English.

We have drawn an invaluable supply of inspiration from many colleagues, friends, and family.

We would like to thank them sincerely for their contributions, patience, and support.

Tony Bannan for his in-depth encouragement and insightful foreword.

Molly Harvey, Jim McNamara, Dominique Mégret, and Paul Woodward for reflecting on our content, giving uncompromising feedback, and ultimately endorsing it.

Andrew Kluge for his case study.

Colin Jefferson and Clive Walden for resolutely proofreading the book and correcting us.

Philip Braunstein and Chris Manka, our partners at **EXP RTEURS** for supporting us throughout the project.

From Laurent to my long-suffering wife and daughter for being there when I needed them.

From John to my late English master at Rugby School, T.D. Tosswill, who said I would never write anything of value.

Endorsements

"A real business life saver. Successful exporting is a must-read book for international business developers. The authors know what they are talking about: they have been developing markets for the last three decades across all five continents. Thanks to the numerous case studies, the book is both instructive and engaging." —**Dominique Mégret, Head of Swisscom Ventures**

"This book takes a practical approach to presenting all the key aspects that need to be considered when launching into international markets. Rooted in the authors' extensive experience, it is written in a down-to-earth and entertaining style that will be more useful to most business people than the many academic and legal volumes written on the same subject. They cut through the sales pitches of the service providers and trade fair organisers who support this industry in a way which won't make comfortable reading to some of those who read the book. It will certainly contribute significantly to avoiding expensive failures." —**Paul Woodward, Former Managing Director of the Global Association of the Exhibition Industry (UFI – Union des Foires Internationales)**

"This book is put together very simply, very easy to follow, and a great tool for anybody contemplating successful exporting." —**Jim Mc Namara, Managing Director, Craghoppers Ltd**

"An amazing no-nonsense compilation of distilled wisdom on how to export successfully. It helps you every step of the way and is full of practical tips and case studies on HOW you can grow your business globally." —**Molly Harvey, FRSA, Chief Executive Officer Harvey Global Ltd**

Foreword

When Laurent Houlier and John Blaskey asked me to write the foreword to this book, I was more than a little puzzled. Why me? What do I know that makes my perspective worth listening to? Like many businesspeople, I have been happily occupied, for quite some time now (since about 1988) in exporting my products and services to countries far and wide, some close neighbors with a broadly similar outlook, some far away with very, very different cultures and values. And, like many of my fellow travelers, it has become relatively routine to do deals and agree contracts in the United States, France, Spain, Germany, China, Russia, Taiwan, India, Japan, Indonesia, Malaysia, South Korea … to name only some. It has, in that tired old phrase, become the norm. But, when I paused for a moment and reflected upon this fact, I realized that it is anything but the norm. Usually, the only way to get to work in so many countries is to join the armed forces, and there is a downside to that, you risk being shot at.

Even in this global age, where economies are increasingly interconnected and interdependent, it is still a minority of businesses that take the plunge. And, here is the thing: there is a whole world of opportunity out there, literally, if only you know how to navigate to it. That is what this excellent and very readable little book is all about.

For the exporter, the desire to explore is self-explanatory, the means and equipment comprise the funds and the toolkit, the documents, the guaranteed payment mechanisms, credit insurance, standards guidelines, and regulatory processes. These latter items sound onerous, but they are not. They are simply the nuts, bolts, and seals of your exporting kit. Practical help and assistance with this stuff are readily available from Chambers of Commerce and business clubs. Even your business's bank will offer to help, but as we all know, they do not do anything for free. However, although getting all of these matters straightened out is both necessary and a little boring, this in itself will not ensure you have a successful outcome. For that you need to think about the less obvious things, the little tricks and *hacks* that enable you to leave your competitors behind.

Laurent and John will enlighten you on some of the subtleties needed to successfully win export business, but also guide you in getting the best from the activities that are often run in parallel with but separated from an export strategy, such as customizing your website for different readers, e-commerce techniques, optimizing your exhibition planning and execution, working with sales agencies and distributors, and even establishing in-country facilities. Throughout, they present their advice in a reader-friendly style, always based on real-world experience and examples, and even provide checklists to help you plan and prioritize.

Now is the time. Take the plunge.

Tony Bannan, OBE, Chief Executive Officer Precision Technologies Group (PTG)/Director CHMTI (Chongqing, China), Engineer, Traveler, Exporter

Preface

What This Book Will Do for You

This book identifies key dangers, posing strategic practical questions, which you need to consider when you decide to export seriously.

You are an existing or would-be entrepreneur. You study business. You are time-poor. You are ambitious. You want to expand your business globally. You want to spread your risk. And, you want to add value to your present or future organization. Your mind is veering toward exporting.

You know this cannot happen accidentally or incidentally. You need a strategy and rapid access to practical reliable information in order to negotiate your way through the barriers to success.

Your business is or will be unique. Your export strategy needs to be equally unique. Of course, the decisions you take have to be tailored to your business, its scale, and your declared ambitions.

We draw on our personal expertise in delivering successful strategies over a combined 75 years of real-life experience. It will either validate or challenge your current approach. This book is not about the technicalities of exporting. It is not about the details of export documentation, import duties, incoterms, choice of logistics companies, and so on. There is already an abundance of relevant published content and resource available.

There is no *one-size-fits-all* recipe for exporting. The belief that you can simply draw on your existing home model or a formula in order to keep it cost efficient without aggravation is in itself a recipe for failure. Your products or services cannot be imposed on a market. Exporting is not a version of *colonialism* or *evangelism*. Exporting successfully depends more than anything on your entire organization embracing the right attitude.

So, what is the right attitude?

We have learned that it must incorporate open mindedness, tolerance, adaptability, willingness to listen, humility, persistence, realism, the ability to look at and understand the intended markets objectively, without being colored by any subjective preconception, only then will you be able to take the right strategic and tactical decisions. Of course, it helps if you have a thirst for knowledge about foreign cultures and people.

If your business has a website, this in itself exposes you to the rest of the world. Social media is largely uncontrollable, and this may result in your being visible far more widely than you ever anticipated. Therefore, whether you are looking for it or not, exporting may be an unavoidable consequence of your everyday local activity.

You are or will probably be exporting already without realizing it, if you are marketing yourselves to any organization that does not know you and needs special consideration, dialect or language, for example, promoting goods or services from Toronto in Montreal, from Geneva in Zürich, from Beijing in Guangzhou, from Boston in San Antonio.

Foreign territories can be the most fascinating places on earth and offer the greatest riches to those who dare, and know how, to explore them. The longer you spend there, the more dangers you will recognize, and the better you will be able to anticipate and deal with them for the greatest returns.

Exporting may appear scary, perhaps because of the fear of not being able to operate easily in a foreign environment. Actually, it is rewarding and accessible to almost anyone, with proper training, research, and planning. The more you practice, the longer you will be able to survive, the more rapidly you will reach your objectives, and the more deeply you will be able to explore these opportunities potentially discovering rich new veins of hidden gold.

We highlight first how time-starved and pressured business owners and directors or managers often ignore holistic strategic thinking in favor of expedient low-cost solutions as a result of rushed decisions.

Based on our genuine observations, we offer practical insights for you to make informed choices and negotiate improved outcomes.

These are followed by a list of pertinent questions challenging you on your approach to making those choices, with a list to remind you to act, making this publication a practical workbook.

Toward the end of each chapter is a deliberately provocative succinct word or phrase to further stimulate your thinking …

So … what kind of an entrepreneur are you or do you aspire to be?

- Are you prepared to move out of your comfort zone?
- Which territories are you going to head for?
- Have you researched the market conditions?
- Where are the most rewarding niches, and how will you reach them?
- Is your organization fit enough?
- Are you well protected?
- Have you got an experienced support team around you?
- Have you decided on your timing?
- What threats will you meet, how will you negotiate them?
- Do you have all the key performance indicators (KPIs) in place to control and measure your progress?
- Will you be able to withstand the pressure?

These are some of the *considerations* to which we refer.

CHAPTER 1

Products and Services: Adapting for Export Markets

You have a range of products or services selling successfully in your home market. You have created a service that, in its design and execution, is unique to your company. Inevitably, you are tempted to assume that your products and services will sell abroad in their current format, you want to exploit any new opportunities without aggravation. You understand that everybody eats to gain energy for the day, works through the day to sustain their families, and sleeps to recharge their human batteries for the next day. So, surely, everybody everywhere looks for the same products, experiences, and lifestyle.

The world is currently comprised of some 195 countries speaking over 7,000 languages, of which 23 are spoken by more than half of the world's population. There are more than 200 commonly identified ethnic groups and around 20 major religions. Add to these the consideration of diverse habitat, climate, and terrain and the notion of gender, which is no longer restricted to male and female, if you include sexual orientation and age groups, you end up with an almost infinite mix of needs, customs, habits, and behaviors.

It is also well established that the impulse to buy generally comes from one or more of three fundamental triggers: how your products and services will save money for your customers, or make their lives easier, or make them feel better.

While your products may be attractive here, how appealing will they be there?

(A) Concept Portability

You have confidence in your products, or services. You know that you have been successful in your home market, despite the normal challenges of business over a number of years. You have a reputation for appropriate products and satisfactory performance within the marketplace. However, you realize that all your sales are coming from a single source. Naturally, you want to spread your risk and, in doing so, add real value to your organization. You prefer not to have all your eggs in one basket. You view export as a potential opportunity to seize additional sales in an uncomplicated way.

To assume that any marketplace is waiting for your products or services is dangerous. It is well known that to "ASSUME makes an ASS of U and ME." Not only do you need to discover where there is a genuine need for your products, but you also need to know who is already in the marketplace occupying the same space with products or services that appear to be similar to yours.

There are historically inherited reputations connected to the country of origin of certain products or services, which endow them with instant credibility and appeal. Think of German engineering, British financial services, American lifestyle, Japanese technology, Italian design, French cuisine, Chinese low-cost production, and so on. While these longstanding generalizations may be undeserved or outdated, they may still today overpower the genuine validity of an original product or service. Your products or services will, therefore, have to be clearly seen to supersede these stereotypes to become successful. And, they may, therefore, need to be adapted.

Have you considered:

- what apparently similar products or services will have been established before your arrival?
- how well your competitors' products are satisfying the local market?
- what original features and benefits your products and services deliver?
- how they chime with local current trends and historical buying patterns?
- whether the market has an appetite for them anyway?
- how you can capitalize on your national reputation?
- how to test conditions to gauge local appeal?

What research have you conducted into the appeal of your products or services abroad?

(B)   Design

You have designed your products, your services, or your processes from years of experience in your own marketplace. You believe in them, and so do your existing customers. Your gut feeling and emotions have supported and guided you. You are now intending to repeat your success abroad, to the same recipe and with the same products.

We have already alluded to the fact that tastes vary infinitely, even within the same nationality, country, or region. The assumption that your mainstream products or services will satisfy any market other than your existing one may amount to flawed thinking. Apart from taking account of normal buying impulses, you need to unearth and be aware of subconsciously inherited local tastes, perceptions, and habits, which could have a detrimental effect on your sales.

You will naturally enhance your understanding about both your future market and your competitors by attending industry tradeshows. Just as important is reviewing the demographics of your targeted territory via relevant trade associations and national commercial representatives. You may discover that there is a need for your products within these markets … but you may find you have to adapt their appearance, for example, color, shape, texture, finish, and so on. If you ignore the issues of redesigning the look of your products for whatever reason, for example, lack of market intelligence, increased costs, insufficient time, or emotional attachment, you do so at your peril.

Have you addressed:

- how to conduct your market research from the point of view of your targeted customers?
- how to assess your competitors' performance?
- feedback from all other sources?
- how your own team will react to necessary changes, adapt, and deliver?
- whether you are in denial?

How objectively will you respond to your market research?

(C)   Sensory Appeal

Your products appeal to your home market and you may be in danger of taking this for granted … without revisiting how they impact on all the senses. You may assume that the way your products feel, taste, smell, or sound, because they are less visible attributes, is inconsequential … and, this may lead you to take shortcuts when presenting your products to prospective channel partners and customers.

Buyer response goes beyond esthetics. Any or all of the other senses could be equally, although more subtly, influential in triggering the impulse to buy.

When your customer groups have the opportunity to experience the touch and feel of your products, they may each have different cultural expectations and reactions, for example, their attitude to synthetic, recycled, or natural materials. Comfort may mean something entirely different to Germans than it does to Italians, firm or soft seating. The same applies to a preference for loose or tailored clothing, cloth or leather car seats, smooth or textured fabrics, wood, tile, stone or carpeted flooring, and so on.

As for what people put in their mouths, your prospective markets may prefer savory flavors to sweet, a bitter taste to aromatic, a crisp texture to soft, spicy to mild, and so on. Culinary considerations in one part of the world may consider various animals a delicacy, for example, dogs, rabbits, horses, turtles, monkeys, frogs, and so on, whereas in another, their consumption would be unacceptable or even illegal. Some societies are innately vegetarian or vegan, and some will include insects in their regular diet. In soft drinks, even the size and strength of the bubbles in your fizzy water may be subject to national preferences, and the sale of wines and spirits may be restricted or illegal, for example, for religious reasons. What about toothpaste and oral medicines? The considerations are endless.

Inescapably connected with food is the influence of aroma, scent, smell, not only from the products themselves, but also from the environment within which it is purchased, the market, the herb garden, the fresh fish slab, the bakery, or the coffee shop. Many buyers are attracted subliminally to the natural smell of various products, for example, leather, soaps, candles, fragrances, incense, flowers, oils, cosmetics, and so on. In many stores, scent is deployed to enhance the atmosphere of their mood and retail experience. Remember the smell of your new car seats when you first sat in them …

With regard to cars, the sounds they make are known to be enhanced to attract a certain type of buyer, for example, at the one end of the scale, the roar of the engine of a high-performance sports car aimed at younger buyers, and at the other, the silence of the electric car aimed at mature buyers. Sounds may be associated with quality, or the lack of it, the reassuring door closing on a luxury vehicle, versus the tinny sound of an inferior household appliance. In some cases, artificial sounds are built into products for psychological acceptability, for example, the click of your android or smartphone camera.

Finally, the sounds associated with any product or service may resonate differently in various countries, for example, the aural logo at the end of your washing machine cycle may be more or less irritating in Europe than in the United States. The science behind in-store *wallpaper* music and how it affects the buying experience and spending impulses is deeply researched, tested, and deployed, for example, a South Korean shopper may react differently to music than a South African in the same store.

What will you do about:

- the sounds associated with your products and services?
- the scent associated with your products and services?
- the taste of your products?
- the touch of your product?

What is the depth of your understanding of local perceptions and sensitivities?

(D)   Technical Compliance

You are satisfied that you have addressed and resolved the *appeal to the senses* of the products and services to be offered abroad. You feel that you are ready to launch . . .

When assessing the technical suitability of your products or services for a particular market, environmental, ethical, legal, and safety interests, all need to be taken into consideration. There is, of course, a need for compliance with the obvious local requirements, for example, voltage, plugs, fire retardancy, product, and packaging recyclability, ingredients, and any integral labeling, which deliver information or instructions. However, the least obvious elements in certain product categories may be aspects of their molecular structure, chemical components, or formulation—and there may be chemicals in the inks or dyes of printed, coated, or impregnated products, which potentially contravene local laws.

Being environmentally friendly is arguably a key concern nowadays in many economies. Product sustainability challenges manufacturers and suppliers from a completely new angle in order to reduce the carbon footprint while remaining affordable.

Any or all of these technical requirements may be enforced through fast ever-changing legislation, demanding that you invest in thorough research and then potentially expensive import certificates, permits, or licenses, and any subsequent inescapable redesign of your products or services.

Have you investigated:

- which technical aspects of your products have to comply with local regulations?
- how safety is regulated in your targeted territory?
- how your machinery or products will behave when operating in extreme conditions?
- which chemicals are permissible?
- what drug or medicine dosages are allowed?
- what religious or cultural restrictions and requirements apply?
- which certificates, licenses, or permits you need?
- how you might have to change, adapt, or redesign your products?

What research in to product compliance have you commissioned?

(E)   Packaging and Labeling

All the investment you have put into the products themselves will inevitably include everything that contains and wraps your product or is attached to it when it reaches your customer. This typically includes all your inner and outer boxing, protective and insulation materials, labeling (presentation, safety, maintenance/care, and so on), swing tags, instruction manuals/CDs/DVDs, and so on.

These of course will have been designed to be effective, compliant, and familiar in your home market. You may want to believe that these will suit your new export territories or hope that they require negligible attention. You may be reluctant to face up to the investment required for an individual country or trading bloc simply to make your product acceptable. Also, regulations are changing constantly.

Inevitably, you will be faced with new costs, which need to be built into your export pricing. You will need to allocate time and resources to conduct the relevant research, ensure compliance and testing, apply for permits, and so on, then translate and redesign whatever is necessary.

Have you considered:

- whether the current style and design of your packaging will appeal to your targeted markets?
- the wording and translation of descriptions, instructions, guarantees?
- how you will handle a growing number of languages in a limited print space?
- the environmental impact? Recyclable, sustainable?
- all aspects of compliance?
- the cost and resources involved?
- who will do the work, and who will pay? You, your channels, or your customers?
- whether the final packaging will be aligned with your brand image and values?

What are the penalties of unsuitable packaging and labeling?

(F)   Pricing

You are probably expecting simply to convert the prices you charge in your local currency to the currency of your prospective buyers—providing you add in the extra costs of transport, duties, and charges. You recognize that your distribution channels will need their margin—although this will raise selling costs. But, you believe that the current unique selling proposition (USP), the differentiator, embodied within your products or services will justify a higher price.

To produce an effective pricing strategy, there are many more variables to take into account. These are not restricted to transport, duties, and charges. Different countries and trading blocs may impose varying import tariffs and taxes. Economic regions like the European Economic Community (EEC), Commonwealth of Independent States, an alliance of former Soviet Republics (CIS), or the US-Mexico-Canada Agreement (USMCA) replacing the 25-year-old North America Free Trade Agreement (NAFTA), to name a few, all have their own import legislation. These constantly change due to political and economic unpredictability in member states.

Some markets will resist paying higher prices locally than those charged in your home market, in particular where these are highly visible online. Others are prepared to pay more for authentic products from established foreign brands with an international reputation.

Export pricing needs to be commercially sensitive, not just cost based. Where products are being retailed to an end consumer, meeting strategic price points is essential to trigger the highest returns. Local competitors may have already established an accepted selling price for products or services similar to yours which you may have to meet or beat. To achieve this, it may be necessary to consider alternative distribution hubs and delivery routes. This requires your awareness of any pricing sensitivities and close collaboration with your chosen channel partners when negotiating terms. To optimize the success and sustainability of your export business, enough margin must be available for all channel partners while allowing the buying price to be attractive to consumers.

NB: There are further considerations, for example, cost of currency transactions, and fluctuations, which are dealt with in a later chapter.

Have you calculated:

- transport and distribution?
- import tariffs, duties, and taxes?
- the implications of local value-added tax (VAT) rates?
- distribution channel margins/commissions?
- meeting or beating your competitors' selling prices?

How viable is your current pricing structure?

Products and Services: Adapting for Export Markets—Key Learnings

1. Identify the original features and benefits of your products and services to establish where there is a genuine need for them. Validate why they will sell from the point of view of your targeted customers.

2. Understand prevalent tastes, perceptions, and habits in local cultures and adapt the look, taste, scent, touch, and sounds of your products or services, where necessary.

3. Ensure that you comply with any local technical regulations and requirements and obtain all necessary certificates, licenses, and permits.

4. Assess the suitability of your packaging and labeling for your targeted markets.

5. Be commercial in your local pricing, whatever your route to market and take account of taxes, tariffs, duties, and so on.

Case Study: Guermonprez, French Manufacturer of Sofas in Europe

Figure 1.1 Sofa representation

Expectation

Guermonprez, a well-established French producer of top-quality contemporary sofas in full grain leathers, decided to sell a range of their products into the largest European markets.

Unforeseen Dangers

The appearance, style, and finish of their existing range proved to be commercial in most key international markets. However, deeper research revealed that acceptability was less down to visible characteristics and far more dependent on invisible factors.

Outcomes

To sell successfully in the German market, which demanded firmer seating than in the original French model, coil springs and higher density foam were offered as options.

The Italian market required the exact opposite, a softer landing, which lead to the addition of a feather layer on top of the standard foam.

The United Kingdom was satisfied with both the appearance and feel of the sofas, but demanded chemical treatment of the foam to comply with stringent fire safety regulations.

Case Study: Western Brands in India

Expectations

Any ambitious company hungry for export growth might consider targeting the emerging BRIC (Brazil, Russia, India, China) countries. These markets offer appetizing opportunities for the shrewd entrepreneur. For example, India is the most populous democracy in the world. Also, English is widely spoken and understood across the Indian subcontinent. Its nominal gross domestic product (GDP) growth rate (according to the International Monetary Fund (IMF)) makes it one of the most attractive economies in the world. It is expected to jump from 7th place in world ranking to 5th in 2019, leapfrogging France and the United Kingdom.

Unforeseen Dangers

It should be remembered, however, that the individual spending power of the population is extremely low. The per capita income was in the region of INR 80,000 (about 1,000 US$, €, and £ depending on exchange rate at the time) per year in 2018. This naturally affects the spending behavior, habits, and expectations of Indian consumers.

Many western products, brands, and services would be unaffordable to the average Indian consumer. Moreover, when customers buy products or services to answer a particular need or solve a challenging problem, they approach them from a different more practical mindset and are differently motivated. For example, where an uninterrupted supply of electricity is taken for granted in developed countries, this is not the case in many parts of India. Designers of products or services, which rely on a constant power supply, have to take this anomaly into account to avoid failure.

Also, businesses expecting to grow through e-commerce in India may be surprised that this channel is struggling, whereas street retailing with personal service is thriving. Passionate recommendations from family and friends, even strangers, count for more in developing trust and buyer loyalty than major advertising campaigns.

In India, convenience, affordability, and cost-effective problem-solving are far more powerful motivators to buy any product or service than any prestige brand advertising.

Outcomes

World famous brand Gillette spent thousands of hours, employed business school graduates, and devoted substantial resources to develop the Vector razor for the mass Indian market. It failed to sell, but not because of its price point. The majority of Indian men need to save water by shaving from a single cup rather than from a running tap. The Vector proved to be difficult to unclog and clean in a cup of water after the first use. Gillette had failed to take account of the local habits and behaviors of the male consumer, which had evolved and were prevalent through practical necessity.

What actions should you take for your business?

Notes

_____

_____

_____

_____

_____

_____

_____

_____

CHAPTER 2

Intellectual Property (IP): Protecting and Leveraging Brands

Your brand is widely recognized and is successful within your current territory. You have developed it over many years in a specific market place so that it enjoys distinction and strength. You believe that it will naturally be accepted and welcomed by your new prospects.

Defining *brand* and its characteristics in a universally acceptable way is close to impossible. What does *brand* actually embody? Is it your company names, product names, logos, trademarks, copyrights, designs, patents, web domains, licenses, franchises, and so on?

The combination of some or all of the aforementioned elements contribute to your unique brand identity and constitute your intellectual property (IP) which, if managed astutely, may become an invaluable company asset. Its value will be quantified according to its innovation, recognition, usage, and its resulting desirability. Therefore, each of these original elements must be carefully managed and protected.

In our experience, a brand is first of all a name that embodies your company's identity and its products or services. Of course, your brand name(s) may be different from the registered name of your company. Brand names are essentially used to differentiate your products and services from those of your competitors, and they are often linked to a logo, which can be used separately from it or together with it. Your brand name may be your logo in itself as depicted by its distinctive type face, font size, punctuation, coloring, and style. Alternatively, it may be a name connected to an additional device, emblem, or symbol.

These represent your brand identity and need to be recognizable in your new target markets. Your brand reputation sets the expectations of prospective customers toward your products and services, their quality, design, price points, applications, benefits, delivery, distribution, communication style, ethics, and values. They are the foundations for your business.

The strength of any brand resides in how much it is valued by your customers, whether or not they are consumers or businesses, end users or channels, … and how well you protect it.

What value does your brand have outside your home market?

(A)   Company and Product Names

You have created, inherited, or bought the names of your company, its products, and services (and inextricably your brand reputation) within your current sphere of influence. You have invested time, money, and energy in securing and maintaining their characteristics. You have every reason to believe that these names will be easily protectable in your new markets … in their entirety.

Registering your company name officially at a registration office, for example, "Companies House" in the United Kingdom, or locally with your Chamber of Commerce, does not grant you any IP rights anywhere. The registration of your company name only protects you from other companies adopting that name within your country. It does not prevent others from selling products or services under your company name anywhere, including your own country. Nor does it automatically confer any protection whatsoever on your brand names, even if they are the same as your company name, and this applies to sub-brands, products, concepts, ranges, derivatives, in-house technologies, processes, and so on.

While text copyright protects originality without significant cost, trademark registrations may be your best recourse. And, they can be registered not only as names or logos, but also as sounds (aural), jingles, or straplines.

You will of course need to consider registering your trademarks in all the relevant categories (or *classes*) within your product range. Internationally, there are 45 classes in total: 34 for products; 11 for services. You need to be clear about the applications of your products or services, then you need to consider what your product actually is (raw material, semifinished, or finished) and, if you are selling a service, its component parts.

Because there is no single worldwide trademark association, registration has to be lodged in each targeted country. However, trademark registration for groups of countries does sometimes exist in customs unions, for example, the EEC via the European Union Intellectual Property Office (EUIPO).

Also, timing is crucial. If you have started selling your products or services under your brand name(s) or trademark(s) in your targeted country, you could discover that these are already held by a local business, not necessarily a competitor, but one that has registered them in the same class (category).

If that business has been using them consistently, this will constitute priority and invalidate your rights. You may have applied to register brand name(s) and trademark(s), but if a local business can prove consistent prior sales of products in the same category under the same name(s), their rights will usually supersede yours.

Apart from this, other organizations may be tracking your business and, anticipating your strategy, register your trademarks in their territory to obstruct you. There are also malevolent *trademark trolls* who professionally target negligent, ignorant, or slow-to-act organizations by monitoring your name searches and then registering your trademarks to coerce you in to buying the title to your own names from them at extortionate prices.

Finally, all registrations have time constraints. While, legally, you do not need to use a trademark *immediately* upon registration, you do within five years. A trademark can be revoked if at the date of filing, there is no genuine intention to use it. This would apply if registration was sought in a class that was never going to be used and would invalidate the entire registration. Practically, you need to have started to sell your products or services under the registered names as early as possible to establish usage and avoid potential legal conflicts. Registrations will all need to be renewed on an ongoing basis, indefinitely, or as is deemed necessary.

You need to think seriously about how, where, and when to invest when registering, managing, and defending your marks at home, and then replicating them in each prospective territory.

Have you considered:

- in which countries, categories, and classes you need protection?
- what budget is needed to protect all your trademarks at home?
- what budget is needed to replicate this activity in each of your prospective territories?
- a carefully timed global strategy to optimize, defend, and future-proof your investment in trademark protection?

How exposed is your company due to inadequate trademark management?

(B)   Brands and Trademarks

You are both satisfied with and proud of the instant recognition your current brand names and trademarks enjoy at home. You know that there is intrinsic value wherever they appear. They are read, pronounced, and understood consistently. They differentiate you clearly from your competitors. They reinforce the promise of your brand. They deliver their own distinct energy.

Now, you need to consider how they might work outside your home market where languages, alphabets, and ideograms are unfamiliar, different, alien. Consider this: you are a Japanese supplier of electronics selling in the United Arab Emirates (UAE), or a Russian distillery selling vodka in Thailand, or a French fashion retailer expanding into China, or a Scottish clothing manufacturer looking to sell in South Korea.

You need to understand the visual and auditory responses that your target population is conditioned to make. This needs thorough research and testing in order to avoid potentially damaging misunderstandings in the reading of and listening to your brand names when written or spoken. Although it may go against the grain to change or amend your brand names, design, or logo in any way, it is imperative to be flexible in order to be commercially effective, without compromising your corporate image and brand values. You also need to be sure that customers in your target market completely understand the meaning of your brand name and its promises.

Have you set about:

- discovering if your brand names are readable locally as they are currently written?
- transposing your brand names in to a different alphabet where necessary?
- expressing your brand names in a different linguistic structure where necessary?
- confirming that the meaning of your amended or translated brand names is not compromised?
- guaranteeing that your brand names are spoken or pronounced as intended?
- ensuring that any redesign of your name or logo does not compromise your brand identity and values?
- registering your amended or translated names logos styles in light of the above?

What sales would you lose where your brand name is incomprehensible?

(C) Patents

Your organization's team has invented unique products and services. Your position in your market resulting from your years of experience and your innovation is so far ahead of your competition that you believe you do not need formal protection. And you know how much this could cost.

Indeed, your innovation and creativity are integral parts of your IP assets. If you have invested significant resources in developing unique technologies, processes, formulae, recipes, or products, you do need to protect them because, of course, you do not want them to benefit other organizations who bypass your consent or do not pay appropriate financial contributions.

Applying to register a patent is no guarantee of its being successfully granted. At the same time, it exposes all the details of your invention or its design. From the moment you go public, it can no longer be patented. Professional searchers constantly troll patent applications on behalf of your known and unknown competitors, with a view to stealing and profiting from your innovation.

It may take up to four years or more from application to the granting of a patent. This in itself is a problem in fast-changing innovative markets. The patent may even have become redundant by the time you are in a position to exploit it. In different territories, there are different time limitations on the life of any patent, after which competitors can legitimately manufacture or provide identical products.

Applications involve significant investment. Your cost commitment is unknown and your patent may ultimately be refused. Even when it is granted, a competitor may recognize its originality and manufacture or market a lookalike product with a slight variation, thereby challenging you to sue them. Your patents need renewing continually and require constant surveillance to protect your rights in your markets. This, then, may become a legal and financial lottery. Experience shows that the organization with the deepest pockets usually prevails.

Have you calculated:

- where to go for the right advice?
- the cost of *not* patenting?
- the potential cost of patenting in all your target markets?
- how to defeat patent pirates?
- what happens after your patents expire?

What are the consequences of not having a comprehensive patent strategy?

(D)   Web Domains

You regard your website as a living, breathing extension of your company's personality, activity, and values. You want to maintain it, manage it, and make it work for you in an increasingly crowded marketplace. Your business organization is professionally run and, to be taken seriously, you have designed a comprehensive website. You expect that this will give you worldwide exposure.

Any website must be properly registered to have any form of presence on the net. Website registration is managed by many individual domain name registrars. They are accredited nonprofit organizations coordinating the domain system globally. However, unlike trademark registration, there are no product or service classifications for websites. So, if a company with the same name as yours, but operating in a different product or service classification, has already acquired the domain you need, you are excluded. You may end up in an auction to acquire the rights to your own domain names.

If you have decided to reach your worldwide audience with your brand name followed by .com (www.yourbrandname.com), remember that this is not country-specific. There are many possible variations of website names, for example, .co.uk for the United Kingdom, .com.cn for China, .fr for France, .ru for Russia, and so on. Within the top-level domain (TLD), category you also need to consider .org, .biz, .net, .info depending on your type of organization, whether it is governmental, not-for-profit, a public limited company (PLC), and so on. To add further complication, there are two other sub-layers of domain category to be considered.

As with trademark registration, you might also be facing *domain squatting* or *cybersquatting.. Cybersquatters* are to Web domains what *trademark trolls* are to trademarks. They exist with the sole purpose of trafficking domain names at extortionate prices. The World Intellectual Property Organization (WIPO) is an arbitration body allowing you as trademark owners to claim back websites that are unlawfully squatted. You may inevitably become embroiled in this distraction from your main business priorities and would incur time and cost in pursuing any action against such pirates.

Have you defined:

- why you need a website?
- how you will register your domain names?
- whether it is an active trading site? Or an informative reference brochure? Or both?
- how you will identify which domain category is most suitable to your business?

What is the real cost of registering and maintaining your domain names globally?

Intellectual Property (IP): Protecting and Leveraging Brands—Key Learnings

1. Treat company and brand names as independent identities when registering them.
2. Optimize, defend, and future-proof the registration of your visual and aural trademarks for greater protection.
3. Validate that your brand names are readable and understood locally as designed.
4. Develop a sustainable and affordable patent registration and protection strategy.
5. Develop a sustainable and affordable protection strategy for Web domain registration.

Case Study: Silver Cross Celebrity Endorsement—United States

Expectations

Up market UK pram and stroller supplier Silver Cross who were exporting substantial quantities of products to the United States published pictures of Jennifer Lopez and Marc Anthony pushing their one-year-old twins in one of their products. Publicity for their brand was clearly the expectation.

Unforeseen Dangers

Most brands nowadays are actively looking for celebrities to use their products and be photographed or filmed with them to be widely publicized. The enthusiasm of Silver Cross for this golden product endorsement and their usage of the photographs for PR occurred without the prior permission of the celebrities.

Outcomes

Jennifer Lopez and Marc Anthony filed a lawsuit in California against Silver Cross for 30 million U.S. dollars, claiming that the photos as published were intended to help sell more product on their website as well as other print and electronic media. This was seen as an illegal attempt to capitalize on their fame without prior contractual consent. The case was ultimately settled out of court for an undisclosed amount.

Case Study: Roger Federer's Initials "RF"

Expectations

In the early stages of his career, Roger Federer registered his full name as a trademark to protect the commercialization of his principle asset, his name and associated reputation.

Unforeseen Dangers

The registration of his full name did not include other variants, for example, his *initials*. It subsequently transpired that, despite his involvement in the product development of his own brand name, he did not own his initials. But, his long-term sponsor, Nike, had designed and registered them in 2010 as a logo successfully representing a clear association with a highly popular sports personality.

Outcomes

When Nike's sponsorship contract with Roger Federer ended in 2018, he was no longer allowed to display his own initials on his person in public!

NB: At the time of writing, Roger Federer is negotiating the return of the now highly valuable rights to his own initials.

Case Study: Nike Brand Registration Conflicts in Spain

Expectations

Based in Beaverton USA and already experiencing world success, Nike Inc. wanted to consolidate their business in Spain and build on their international reputation.

Unforeseen Dangers

An independent Spanish company, Cidesport, had registered trademarks incorporating the name Nike in the apparel category in 1932. They had owned and maintained the rights to exploit the Nike name 32 years before Nike Inc. was born. When Cidesport decided to affirm its rights in the late 1990s, this generated an expensive and lengthy legal dispute. Nike Inc.'s business was constrained for many years to footwear only, which Cidesport did not manufacture.

Around the same time, an independent Spanish company, Campomar, was distributing perfumes as Nike after acquiring a company with the same name. They were promoted as *sports fragrances*. Campomar had successfully registered their trademark with the Office of Patents and Trademarks (OPT). But, Nike Inc. claimed that consumers would be mistakenly led to believe that the brands were connected. Nike Inc. did not sell fragrances, nor did they want this product range to be associated with theirs.

Outcomes

Cidesport: At the end of a 15-year dispute, The Supreme Court eventually ruled in favor of Nike Inc. for its apparel range, citing "lack of real and effective use," confusion on the part of the consumer about where the products originated, and that Cidesport had benefited from Nike Inc.'s worldwide fame. It was extraordinary that the case took so long to resolve, especially because several Spanish courts and European trademark regulators had long recognized Nike Inc.'s full rights to sell apparel under their name in Spain.

Campomar: As for the sports perfumes, the case was settled in favor of Nike Inc. on the basis that Campomar were benefitting unlawfully from Nike Inc.'s global name.

What actions should you take for your business?

Notes

_____

_____

_____

_____

_____

_____

CHAPTER 3

Communication: Bridging Language and Cultural Gaps

You recognize that English is the language of international trade. Consequently, you may be under the impression that if you have a reasonable knowledge of English, you can do business anywhere in the world. That is maybe why you studied English as your second language. You may believe that you can get along with inaccurate pronunciation and incorrect grammar … and if English is your native language, you may think that is all you need.

English is indeed acknowledged as the *lingua franca* for business. *Lingua franca* is defined as a universal language used to communicate between people whose native language is not the *lingua franca*, for example, when an Italian business owner speaks to a Chinese supplier … in English. The development of English as a *lingua franca* is relatively recent and coincides with the emergence of the United States as a superpower after the Second World War and the resulting proliferation of American culture.

English carries the undeserved reputation of being easy to speak. If it is not your mother tongue and you have had to learn English from scratch, you might discover that it is more challenging than expected. The level of learning difficulty actually derives from the origins and structure of your native tongue. A language is spoken before it is written or read. Therefore, in order to be properly understood, sound, tonality, rhythm, emphasis, pronunciation, accent, and so on are all components that need to be conveyed correctly along with the meanings of the words, phrases, or sentences themselves … and your mother tongue may affect your ability to reproduce these elements comprehensively. All these factors contribute to the confidence with which you speak and the authority that you impart.

Beyond the spoken word is written communication. Here, personal interaction is eliminated, and as a result, the nuances of language are lost. Reading a written message is far more susceptible to misinterpretation. To counter this, an in-depth knowledge of the grammar, syntax, vocabulary, and idioms of a language is essential to avoid any misunderstandings.

What attention have you paid to being understood?

(A)   Englishes

You may take for granted that there is only one English language and it is universally understood in the world of business. You may assume that your own staff and those in your prospects' organizations will manage to make themselves understood. And, if English is your mother tongue, you may think you are home and dry.

There are certain countries, for example, The Netherlands, Sweden, Denmark, where most of the population will speak reasonable English, probably because of the rare usage of their own language anywhere outside their homeland and, perhaps because of their incessant exposure to original English or American media content (TV, cinema, Internet, and so on) broadcast with subtitles.

While English may be spoken to some degree internationally, it is not necessarily practiced at the levels required to conduct business transactions. Only about 40 percent of the European Union (EU) population knows enough English to hold a conversation. Statistically, in countries where it is not their mother tongue, younger people are far more likely to have studied English than their elders. While there may be more fluent English speakers in the upper levels of corporate management, in the rest of the organization, a larger majority of people may be less able, or too shy, to speak English adequately. Those employees who do not have a working knowledge of English may face significant career obstacles when they want to progress to top management. After all, they may have been hired originally more for their management skills and experience than their command of English.

Your prospects, wherever they are located in the world, will undoubtedly have been exposed to different types of English, each with its own idiosyncrasies. These include Irish, Scottish, Welsh, American, Canadian,

Australian, Indian, and any of the versions spoken in the other 50 or more countries where English is an official language. Low-cost call centers located in poor or underdeveloped regions of the world are often used to communicate with consumers despite their almost incomprehensibly accented English. The vocabulary, context, references, meanings, idioms, and accents are differently interpreted and acted upon by each of the 1.5 billion people (20 percent of the world's population) who speak English, even the 360 million people for whom it is their mother tongue.

Doing business in English is not just about the spoken word. The nuances of body language, the effect of unfamiliar pronunciation, the impact of the speed and tone of the spoken word, all need to be taken in to account.

Written communication between you and your customers is yet another two-way challenge. As a result, your customers' and prospects' comprehension of content published in English may be variable and unsafe. This may adversely impact their understanding of, and reaction to, your leaflets, catalogs, website, promotional media, and so on and crucially your business forms.

Have you identified:

- who in your organization can best communicate in written English?
- who has the best command of spoken English?
- how effective is your communication (your commercials, websites, presentations, documentation, and so on), when expressed abroad in *your* English?
- what level of understanding of English exists in your prospects' company?
- what to do if English is not understood?

What opportunities might be lost when you rely on your English?

(B) Translation

You have heard that there is a wide choice of translators (or interpreters), text translation companies, freelance translators, translation software, and

now free Internet translation service providers, like Google translate …
to name but a few. You have a restricted budget. You are under time
pressure. You are tempted to go for what appears to be a quick, easy, and
cost-effective option. If English is not understood by your target customer and you are on a budget, you might be drawn to using a *translation
software* or an interpreter.

You may consider that current translation software is the panacea. It
delivers results mechanically and is usually available free of charge from
main search engines. This may be adequate for simple routine questions,
for example, details of a trip. However, you need to validate that this software would also work for your website, catalog, leaflets, documentation,
and any promotion or advertising that requires sophisticated language.
Literal translation may either not be understood by your customers, or
engage them, if it lacks the emotional dimension. There may be nuances
and moods, which you need to convey using, for example, rhyme, sar-
casm, humor, metaphor, context, drama, and so on. You need to be …
human, not a robot, to *CAPTCHA* them. Translation software is unable
to articulate the second- or third-level meanings, that is, the emotional
intelligence, behind words, phrases, or sentences. Actually, there are many
native speakers who might not *get it* either … possibly through a lack of
education or a disconnect with current culture.

Naturally face-to-face business conversations in a language you do not
speak well enough, or at all, may prompt the services of an interpreter.
A full understanding of what your potential partners wish to convey (or
conceal) requires more than mere verbal interpretation. It is well known
that there are three different components of communication: only 7 percent of the meaning is transmitted through words, 38 percent is through
voice tone, and 55 percent comes through body language. Any incongru-
ence between these three components may reveal a hidden agenda in a
negotiation where authenticity and trust are paramount.

Remember, there are words that are so universally used that any literal written translation may confuse their meaning rather than making
their understanding clearer. The word *marketing* may be considered jargon, but it is globally understood and accepted worldwide. Your teams
will also use industry jargon, that is, words and phrases that are often
untranslatable.

In the final analysis, if you do not have an in-depth command of the language in to which your words are to be translated, it will be challenging for you to confirm the accuracy of the translation, so that it genuinely conveys the original authentic meaning.

Are you ensuring that:

- you have chosen the correct mix of translation facilities?
- that the words translated into your customer's language express your intended meaning without misleading inferences?
- your jargon and technical terms are being accurately translated?
- your face-to-face communications are conveyed accurately and understood by the other party?
- your interpreter has the emotional intelligence to report any incongruency from the other party and you understand their true intent?
- you have trusted communicators?

What are the visible and invisible costs of misinterpretation?

(C)   Cultures

You are aware that absorbing foreign languages is an integral part of going global and you know you can recognize and adapt to the differences in international behaviors and cultures. You have taken on board that globalization ideally requires your company to be perceived as local, not *foreign*. You take for granted that there is genuine goodwill between you and your prospective customer(s), and that there needs to be two-way flexibility concerning the inescapable cultural divide. When negotiating, you will of course be aware that this flexibility may be hostage to the commercial interests of either partner.

Your conditioning, past experience, and inherent emotions subconsciously affect your personal interactions, irrespective of where and with whom you are aiming to do business. Exporting requires this subconscious behavior to be adjusted consciously to the sensitivities and judgments of those in your prospective marketplace. Cultural bullying (imposing or persuading people of the superiority of your own behaviors) needs to be recognized and handled sensitively so as not to damage your developing relationship.

You and your business partners will inevitably be judging each other's behaviors subconsciously and consciously. The danger is to judge, or be judged, adversely by your prospects and customers due to a possible lack of emotional intelligence, education, or awareness of each other's objectives. Confronting challenges and being aware of the different emotional behaviors of foreign counterparts are at the heart of potential success in your new export business.

Studies have been conducted that point to commonly accepted traits in national behaviors. It is helpful to know that those from different cultures will interact more or less intensely to disagreement, for example, while Asian people tend to avoid direct confrontation in discussion or negotiations, often motivated by the fear of *losing face.* In Mandarin Chinese, there is no specific word that matches the meaning of "no" in English. The words to use will depend on the context and grammar of the question. Other nationalities like the British hide contradictory opinions believing they are being *diplomatic.* At the other end of the spectrum, most European populations communicate in a more straightforward manner, for example, in Germany, it is acceptable to be more direct in any disagreement either with your customers or your superiors. There is an undeniable connection between the intensity of passion and emotions with which people converse and their exposure to regular sunshine. Italians will usually be seen as flamboyant whereas Russians are typically more introvert.

Despite well-observed common traits within national behaviors, your business relationships will be with individuals who may not fit perfectly into these stereotypes. Their life history, education, ethnicity, and business experience will have influenced them uniquely, as will yours. Finding the nonjudgmental middle ground of reciprocated understanding is fundamental to sustaining mutually rewarding commercial relationships.

Have you paid attention to:

- your or their first impressions?
- where or how you will meet (video or telephone conference, their premises, your premises, neutral territory)?

- who is who, by seniority (influential outsider, owner, director, manager, observer, support, and so on) and title, ally or enemy?
- who does what, by designation, ally or enemy?
- who makes the relevant decisions?
- greeting, business cards, dress code?
- political correctness, manners, and traditions?

Will you jeopardize a deal by being out of touch with local culture?

(D)   Presentation

When thinking about your business imagery and messaging, your brand proposition, and your communication style you may want to believe that *one size fits all.* You have created a library of still shots and video footage at substantial expense, and you may expect to use them in your business media as they are. You may be tempted to avoid dealing with the many subjective cultural responses that your presentations will inevitably provoke.

This subject is far more complex than it appears. Every aspect of your communications will be scanned subconsciously and interpreted reactively by everyone who views them. They deliver much more than just audio and visual messaging. This is especially sensitive when you are presenting in person. The success of your impact relies on the engagement by your audience with your layout, imagery, font, style, color, sound track, and voice whenever you communicate. It applies to your logos (audio and visual), leaflets, catalogs, websites, social media, illustrations, videos, background music, business cards, promotions, trade shows, packaging, e-mails, and so on—in fact, every aspect of your corporate presence.

Languages, when spoken, do not have an orientation. When they are written, the visual layout of text needs to sync with the way the reader has been conditioned to read, taking into account the differences between alphabets, ideograms, syllabic characters, and so on. Some languages are read horizontally from left to right, including those with roots in Latin, (Modern) Greek, Cyrillic, Indic, and Southeast Asian, for example, the modern languages of the Americas, Europe, India, and Southeast Asia. Others are written and read from right to left, still horizontally, for example, Arabic, Persian, Hebrew, and Urdu. Ideographic languages, for example, Japanese, Chinese, and Korean, are more flexible. They can be read in lines from top to bottom and left to right but also in columns, in which case, they are read right to left, top to bottom . . . and from a Western perspective, back to front!

Greek

**Horizontal
left to right
top to bottom**

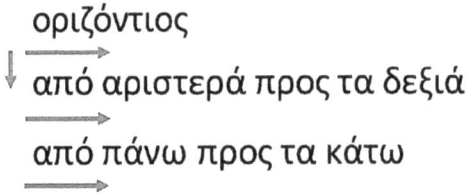

οριζόντιος

από αριστερά προς τα δεξιά

από πάνω προς τα κάτω

Figure 3.1 Direction of reading Greek

Arabic

**Horizontal
right to left
top to bottom**

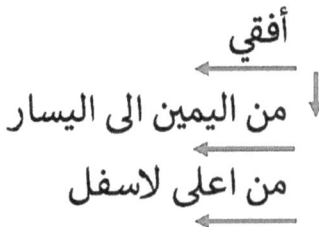

أفقي

من اليمين الى اليسار

من اعلى لاسفل

Figure 3.2 Direction of reading Arabic

Chinese

**Horizontal
left to right
top to bottom**

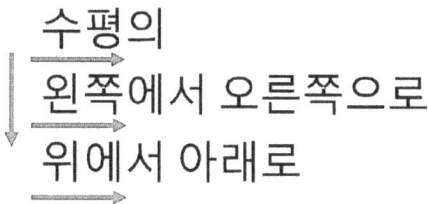

**Vertical
top to bottom
right to left**

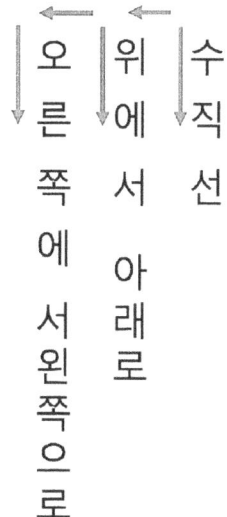

橫
左到右
從上到下

右
到
左

從
上
到
下

垂
直

Figure 3.3 Direction of reading Chinese

Korean

**Horizontal
left to right
top to bottom**

**Vertical
top to bottom
right to left**

수평의
왼쪽에서 오른쪽으로
위에서 아래로

오
른
쪽
에
서
왼
쪽
으
로

위
에
서
아
래
로

수
직
선

Figure 3.4 Direction reading Korean

Depending on the language family that is adopted, the overall appeal of any material can be seriously affected by the way the text is laid out.

As to visual imagery, a simple concept, for example the satisfaction or delight delivered by your products or services has to be carefully presented so as not to offend cultural sensitivities. This can be expensive if your existing material is not suitable. For example, conveying happiness through videos or still shots of people dancing may seem straightforward enough and universally acceptable, but your imagery may offend in countries where dancing has religious significance. Equally, the selection of accompanying vocal or instrumental music may prove to be a further challenge.

Worldwide responses to a simple concept, for example *having a cup of tea* can vary enormously according to cultural conditioning and depends on imagery and presentation. Taking tea in Japan (powdered green tea or *matcha*) can be a religious ritual (tea ceremony or *Way of Tea* in Japanese *chanoyu*) typically experienced in a traditional tearoom with tatami floor, with traditional sweets to balance the bitter taste of the tea. In the United Kingdom, a mug of tea (from a tea bag) invariably needs milk. In China, tea enjoys a vintage, like French wine, tea (from leaves) is taken in small cups constantly refilled, and the experience is usually shared. Thailand's tea culture involves a distinctly amber-colored iced tea, which is a blend of Ceylon or Assam, and is flavored with sugar, condensed milk, and various spices usually served on ice in a tall glass.

These differences can be extended to coffee, hot chocolate, alcoholic drinks (cocktails or shots), and virtually all culinary traditions. Ignoring them in your presentation of any product or service, along with any seasonal considerations relating to opposite hemispheres, may have an adverse effect on the response to what you are aiming to communicate.

Are you conversant with:

- which way your prospect reads?
- whether your trade name or logo is readable locally?
- how Asian prospects will read websites with Western orientation, and vice versa?

- where the high-impact point is on a magazine page advert in your target country?
- where the *call to action* button should appear on your foreign website?
- seasonal demands when selling in a different hemisphere?
- the backgrounds and activities in your imagery that connect with local culture?
- whether your communications are politically correct locally and globally?
- whether your messaging connects culturally and emotionally with your targets?
- whether your presentation will generate the desired response or reaction?

What is the impact of misdirected audio-visual imagery?

(D) Humor

You may believe that humor will help to charm, tease, seduce, and amuse your audience in order to draw their attention to your products or services. Perhaps, you think that your sense of humor is universal. You expect it to deliver the same reaction abroad as it does with your home audience.

People *buy* people, before they buy products or services. Assuming that everybody enjoys humor, your sense of humor may not be theirs. The context might not be appropriate or timely, even within regions of your own country.

Firstly, if humor is not natural to you, you could be seen as fake, not authentic, when you attempt to introduce it, and this can affect your credibility. Secondly, there is an inherent distinction between verbal and visual humor, in that what you say and what you transmit through your body language and gestures must once again be in sync to be convincing. Thirdly, the humor you use in business should always be self-deprecatory: it should neither be directed against your prospects nor devalue or demean your own products and services.

Humor is a double-edged sword, which must be handled very sensitively whenever it is used in published texts, catalogs, websites, social media, printed or televised advertising campaigns, and especially during face-to-face business conversations or presentations. Remember: to be effective, humor must draw on life experiences, social relevance, and references that are common to all parties.

Humor in corporate communications can be a nightmare for any marketing department, which needs to make it universally acceptable. There are many well-documented horror stories of campaigns incorporating humor, which, unfortunately, deliver highly effective responses in one country and sabotage their proposition in others.

Are you sure that:

- employing humor is the correct approach?
- your sense of humor will cross borders effectively?
- you are not offending cultural, religious, or personal sensibilities?
- you are not devaluing your own products or services?

Can you afford to compromise your brand through misconstrued humor?

Communication: Bridging Language and Cultural Gaps—Key Learnings

1. Test the assumption that your foreign markets will understand *your* English and validate the effectiveness of all your communications carefully.
2. Wherever *your* English is not suitable, translate authentically into the local language or dialect and have it validated locally.
3. Configure your presentations in alignment with the reading orientation of your audience, and adjust them to be correctly seen, read, and understood.
4. Make sure your target audiences are universally engaged by all your communications, and you are culturally in sync with them.
5. Be accurate when using local jargon or technical terms; be mindful when you use humor.

Case Study: Exporting Japanese *Manga* to the West

Figure 3.5 Manga comic book

Expectations

Japanese publishers of Manga comic books wanted to exploit their global potential in the West, the largest market in the world for this genre. They know that they have to make this unique art form acceptable and under-standable to readers accustomed to a completely different orientation and narrative flow, without compromising the original art creation and story.

Figure 3.6 Manga pages read the Japanese way

A native of Japan would read a traditional Manga book back to front, top to bottom, right to left.

Unforeseen Dangers

If the original traditional Manga layout is retained, where in Japan the content is scanned back to front, top to bottom, right to left, and the text is translated in to the language of the target *Western* market, readers would lose some of the original sense, style, and emotion from the unfamiliar flow. This is because the reading direction of the Western text will desynchronize with the illustrations.

It may otherwise be decided simply to mirror the original pages (known as *flipping*) to accommodate the habits and comfort of the Western reader in a cost-effective way. However, this would result in a loss of authenticity and homogeneous reading flow. The text may conflict with the illustrations, for example, a character pointing to their left when the text indicates an item to their right, words or names on billboards appearing backward, and so on.

Figure 3.7 Manga pages as read in the West

Japanese Manga book "flipped for Western readers to read front to back; left to right; top to bottom".

Outcomes

In the absence of the perfect solution, both of the aforementioned strategies, requiring varying degrees of compromise, were adopted by publishers who had spotted an opportunity. They saw that the popularity of animated Japanese cartoons broadcast on European TVs in the 1970s, had stimulated an insatiable thirst for Japanese comic art among youngsters. This set the scene for the arrival of Mangas, which enjoyed outstanding success in Europe.

NB: How could this adjustment be applied for the reading of a web page, a catalog, or a magazine by Western companies wishing to trade in Japan, China, or South Korea?

Case Study: HSBC Promoting Their Banking Services Globally

Expectations

HSBC Bank, based in the United Kingdom, had conducted a successful promotional campaign in the United States based on a particular strapline. They then decided to adopt the same message globally, assuming that it would be universally effective.

Unforeseen Dangers

The campaign featured the strapline *Assume nothing*. This concise sentence with its subtle message is so succinct that when translated literally, it loses its original meaning. In many countries, the understanding of the direct translation was *Do nothing*. As a call to action with the aim of inviting prospects to bring their private banking to HSBC, the resulting translation negated the bank's intent, which was the acquisition of many new customers and the building of trust.

Outcomes

Having investigated the failure of the original campaign when translated into foreign languages, HSBC decided to invest in a new 6.8-million-pound rebranding exercise as *The world's private bank* to correct the client inertia that had resulted.

Case Study: The Last Costa Concordia Cruise—Italy

Expectations

In today's fast-growing cruise industry, with ever larger vessels (hotel ships) and an unlimited mix of staff and passenger nationalities, language is an increasingly sensitive challenge. While there has been an attempt at international legislation to require proficiency in English for mariners, compliance is the responsibility of shipping companies or their contractors. Checks are rarely conducted, as it is costly to hire staff with requisite language skills. It is assumed that language barriers will be overcome.

The modern cruise ship Costa Concordia was sailing on a seven-day Mediterranean cruise with 3,206 passengers and 1,023 crew members on board, with a total of 66 nationalities. The background nationalities of the crew alone numbered 38 from as diverse countries as Peru, Russia, China, The Philippines, Spain, and India, with an Italian captain and officers.

To execute an unscheduled sail-past salute, the vessel deviated from its charted course and sailed closer to the Isola del Giglio Island than the original route. Sail-past salutes are not unusual in this industry, and Costa ships had drawn nearby in the past with no problem.

Unforeseen Dangers

The official working language on this ship was Italian, and English was also widely used. In fact, although all the staff spoke at least basic English, most spoke no Italian.

When instructions were given to navigate the sail-past salute, misunderstandings occurred during compensating maneuvers, which were needed as soon as imminent danger was identified.

It transpired that the Master's orders were spoken in English, but were not consistently understood by the Indonesian helmsman.

The Bulgarian first engineer failed to understand orders given in Italian during the ensuing emergency.

The boatswain issued orders in Italian and English to the South American crew who had hardly any knowledge of either language.

The safety trainer reported that all training activities were usually carried out in English, despite an obvious lack of comprehension from many of the crew.

Outcomes

On January 13, 2012, the Costa Concordia struck an underwater rock, ran aground, and overturned with the loss of 32 lives.

The lack of understanding of the initial navigational orders combined with chaotic communication in executing emergency procedures clearly contributed to exacerbating a disastrous result. The crew had been hired with a view to cost savings where communication skills, languages, and safety procedures were not valued as priorities.

Apart from the incalculable cost in human life, the company suffered financial losses of around two billion U.S. dollars, more than three times the original cost of the ship.

What actions should you take for your business?

Notes

_____

_____

_____

_____

_____

_____

CHAPTER 4

Tradeshows: Optimizing and Measuring Performance

As a would-be exporter, you might consider exhibiting at an international show in the belief that it will automatically bring in additional business. You have been approached by your trade association, professional body, or an independent organizer to take space at a forthcoming show. The event sales staff tell you that your presence is crucial to your future. All your competitors are exhibiting. Most key decision makers will attend. Your success is guaranteed. You are led to reflect on what people would think if you were *not* there. You are a regular exhibitor and believe it has always worked for you. As a result, you feel you have to be there.

There is no doubt that live marketing is back if you are selling business-to-business (B2B). Despite the advent of social media, the Internet, and online trading, meeting prospects, and customers face-to-face at an appropriate event may be the most powerful way to initiate, develop, and commercialize a business relationship for the long term. However, there are many alternatives: you may create your own roadshow, master class, *lunch and learn*, and so on; you may participate in a tradeshow, conference with a showcase or at a direct-to-consumer (D2C) fair or event, where you may literally sell your products or services from your stand.

There are a number of shows, fairs, and festivals which combine B2B and D2C audiences. You need first to decide who you really want to speak to and what you want to say to them.

New shows in emerging industries are springing up and replacing older shows in saturated marketplaces. Organizers still have to deal with the fact that they retain too few exhibitors from one edition to the next. Exhibitors may be reluctant to return because they are uncertain about whether or not they have been successful enough to justify their costs by measuring what prospective results they have actually achieved.

What are the consequences of exhibiting to the wrong audience?

(A) Traffic

You expect that taking space at a professionally organized conference or tradeshow will put you in front of a large number of prospects who you would not otherwise meet, invited, and delivered by the organizers. You assume that, because you have invested a significant amount, the organizers will deliver everyone to you. You may believe that there is little promotion to be done on your part.

In order to cut costs, some organizers are tending to merge apparently complementary shows, with the result that the audience will not be as specific as you may expect. Also, extraneous circumstances such as political disturbance, the weather, industrial action, and so on can all reduce your audience quantity and dilute its quality. These factors are usually beyond your control. Researching every aspect of the event is essential because buying space at an unproven show, or one that is losing the quality and quantity of its audience, can be fruitless and, therefore, wasteful.

It is misguided to assume that professional event organizers will automatically deliver your audience. Even if they do, you still have to attract enough of the right prospects into your space and engage them in a meaningful conversation leading to the next stage in your buying cycle. Failing to target, promote, invite, and engage with your clearly defined audience may deliver a far from respectable return on investment from the show.

In any event, your regular business will be disrupted in the run-up to the show, your teams will experience pressure at the event itself, and you will be further tested when following through new bona fide prospects afterward.

Have you asked:

- how long has the show been established?
- if the show is an amalgamation of previously separate shows?
- how aligned is the invited audience with your own targets?

- how will you stand out and draw customers and prospects in to your space?
- how will you filter real prospects from time wasters, or spies?

How much are you ready to gamble on your exhibition audience?

(B)   Decision Makers

You have decided to exhibit. You are satisfied that the organizers will deliver your audience in terms of quality and quantity. You naturally anticipate that the key decision makers will be there, come past your stand and stop.

Key decision makers may visit events because they wish to know about new industry trends, innovative products and services, who is driving their industry, and what you have to offer.

Business owners, senior directors, and buyers may already have seen their most important suppliers prior to a show. They may prioritize visiting exhibitors with whom they have important supply issues to resolve (*complaints*) certainly the least desirable conversations that you want to have on your stand. Ideally, they will have identified those exhibitors offering genuine and relevant innovation, as well as those who can play a significant part in their growth. It is important to remember that they usually have a limited time and attention span.

As a result, the tendency today is for senior executives and decision makers to send lower-ranking managers to identify potential new suppliers and then report back. These prospectors are unlikely to have the authority to commit in any way to a future appointment, which is ultimately what you need.

Well in advance of the show, you need to give those with decision-making authority a compelling reason to visit you and, wherever possible, set up a timed appointment.

Have you researched:

- the status or positions of show visitors in your target categories?
- the percentage of show visitors at this level?

- a compelling reason for the right prospects to visit your stand?
- how you will invite and engage them?

What price not hooking top buyers?

(C)   Expectations

You have booked a space at your first exhibition or re-booked at a show you have already attended. Your sales people have persuaded you to be there . . . reminding you that your key competitors have taken space. Of course, you know that the show is a great place to meet your distributors and customers . . . you can network. You expect to sign enough orders at least to break even on costs.

Many exhibitors measure their success at a tradeshow, conference, or fair with the self-deluding assessment "I think we probably broke even" to justify their attendance and investment. *Breaking even* should never be reward enough for the months of preparation, input of energy, allocation of resources, and disruption to your regular business. Rarely are new contracts initiated, developed, and signed at a B2B tradeshow. You seldom have the time and resources to credit check or evaluate prospects and take an order at a tradeshow. Generally speaking, where a contract is signed at a show, this is essentially a staged public relations (PR) exercise and is the result of much pre-event negotiation and preparation. It is a brand profile exercise.

Furthermore, when showcasing your products or services in a marketplace that features your perceived competitors, there will be considerable reluctance on the part of prospects to buy from you until they have reviewed all their options. While these potentially long-term customers may not actually sign a contract at the show, you will have the opportunity to capture all their relevant data to facilitate any future engagement.

Crucially, you must create compelling and practical reasons for serious prospects to engage with you again.

Have you decided:

- who is most likely to sign orders at the show and how you will handle the process?

- how you will persuade prospects to engage with you again?
- how to measure the success of the show?

What are you losing by weak prospect follow-up?

(D)   Staffing

You have decided that the main aim of exhibiting is to meet your global distributors, agents, wholesalers, and customers. You will save money in the long run by reducing individual country missions and sales visits. You may even expect to write some new orders. You will be networking. You conclude that the best people to staff your stand are your regional or territory sales representatives or agents.

Your show objectives may include prospecting for new customers or partners, gathering marketing intelligence on trends and available projects, raising the profile of your brand, and delivering a total experience of your organization. In this case, you may need a different team mix. This should include staff who have the skills to perform the roles of prospectors (*hunters*), brand ambassadors, presenters, and data managers, not just sales people.

Sales representatives may justify their presence at a tradeshow, fair, or conference "to meet existing customers." But, this is unnecessary unless they write specific orders that they would not have otherwise secured. In effect, their on-stand presence means that they are absent from their day-to-day responsibilities. They will be working in an alien environment, but are still expected to be effective, possibly in a foreign language. Inevitably results will be at best random.

The visible costs of having any or all of your sales team present on your tradeshow stand, or at your conference, can be calculated. If you add in to the calculation their salary packages, travel, accommodation and entertainment, and so on, the true cost is a substantial component of your overall exhibition investment. Moreover, the invisible costs, that is *the opportunity costs*, of your representatives' absence from their regular duties are difficult if not impossible to calculate, but they are real.

NB: Tradeshows are principally marketing. Marketing is your *flirting*. Selling, your *dating*, comes later.

Have you decided:

- whether the show is principally a marketing or a selling exercise?
- who performs which roles on your stand (engaging, entertaining, educating, collecting data)?
- if your aims are to attract new customers, service existing customers, or both?
- what market intelligence and contact data you wish to gather?
- whether your representatives or agents should be there?

How can you afford to take your representatives off the road?

(E)   Literature

You are exhibiting at a key industry show. You have observed over the years most exhibitors distributing literature on their stands, in giveaway bags, and randomly on the show floor. You may have pressured your marketing department to produce new brochures and catalogs *in time for the show*. You expect the collateral, even with potential misprints and short-term information, to do the work for you.

You will need to design the content to promote your brand or sell individual products or services or both. The literature may have to be printed in many languages.

In reality, the majority of brochures collected by visitors at a show are dumped. Nobody wants to carry them these days. At the end of most tradeshows, you will see piles of promotional literature discarded by visitors. Also, as stands are dismantled, there are significant numbers of boxes of them left behind by exhibitors who are too tired to take them back to their office, which flies in the face of current sustainability behavior.

If a genuine prospect (not one of your competitors) has visited your stand, expressed their interest in what you offer, picked up your brochure, and given you their card, you would naturally call them afterward to follow up. However, their response may simply be "I have your brochure, I will contact you if I need you." By letting them have your literature you have in effect removed a key reason for them to engage with you again.

Carefully crafted feedback forms, contact data capture technology, and market surveys have been proven to be more powerful than printed marketing material in actively progressing a lead from a show to a commitment to purchase.

Have you asked yourself:

- how likely are you to risk educating your competitors?
- what cost effective data capture technology could you use?
- how you will convert requests for catalogs or brochures in to meaningful leads?
- how planet-friendly are you?

What is the real cost of impotent promotional literature?

(F) Presentation

You are exhibiting at a show. Your natural inclination is to display your full range of products or services to ensure that no sales opportunity is missed. You may be buying in to the organizers' and contractors' promotional myth that *size matters*, and that you now need one of the larger stands, a grander construction, or even an expensive *double decker*.

This delusion of grandeur may result in the need for more stand staff, resources, and control. The organizers may site you in a less desirable location, perhaps at the entrance to the show, where visitors typically walk past you. You may be constantly developing and introducing new products and services. So, it will be more and more difficult to prioritize which of them are going to appeal to the show audience. You may have to produce expensive new samples or prototypes for a show. Transporting, installing, and embedding machinery is also risky. And, displaying everything in an organized and attractive way is always challenging.

These considerations demand differing strategies, which can sometimes be combined. You may wish to sell your ranges to existing customers and seriously interested prospects, there and then, on the stand. This requires a discreet space, a controlled visitor journey, and experienced sales staff.

Equally, you may wish to tell the story of your brand to a wider unknown audience in a way that leaves them wanting to learn more. This would require a dramatic and consistent presentation of your style, brand values, credentials, and partnership opportunities. Tell the stories of how you will benefit your prospects when they buy from you. Rather than showing visitors what a product is, tell them what it does . . . benefits rather than features. This constitutes a different approach aiming at a more in-depth conversation later to drive future business. These two strategies demand separate visitor journeys and management.

Have you defined:

- whether you are principally exhibiting to sell products or market your brand?
- … or both?
- which are your outstanding signature products or services?
- a clear engagement strategy?
- how you will leave customers and prospects wanting to meet you again?

What is the cost to your reputation of an inadequate stand?

(G) ROI and ROO

Return on investment (ROI) and return on objectives (ROO)

You have just exhibited. You believe you were successful. Compliments were paid about the look of your stand and your brand. Your products were well received. Promises were made, and you networked with many like-minded colleagues from your industry. You are anticipating a substantial return on your investment. The event organizers visited your stand on the last day of the show with reports of increased attendance, better visitor quality, and urgent new demand for space. You are tempted to commit for the next edition.

Euphoria may now affect your objectivity. As a professional entrepreneur or manager, you would measure every aspect of your business performance: sales, gross margin, costs, profit, future prospects, asset value, future investment, human capital, and so on. Strangely, the same discipline and evaluation are rarely applied to exhibiting, or indeed, to any live *face-to-face* marketing activity.

When it comes to tradeshows, or indeed any form of live marketing, professionals often fail to determine what they want to measure in the first place, and then how to do it. The perception is that live marketing cannot be measured.

Contrary to received wisdom, results are measurable in the marketing world. Promotional media are regularly measured. Search engine optimization (SEO) is deployed to enhance the success of your website. The reach of your social media is also carefully monitored. Percentages of response to mailing campaigns are scrutinized. You collect data and act on them accordingly for the future. Logically, you should apply the same rigor to your exhibiting activity in order to rate your success accurately and benchmark your performance for the future.

What data are you going to collect and evaluate:

- the average annual or lifetime value of your customers?
- the number of visitors to your stand (more or less than last time)?
- the authority and quality of your prospects?
- the number of requests for future meetings?
- market intelligence: trends, opinions, available projects, competitor performance?
- the effectiveness of your brand messaging?
- all your visible and invisible costs?
- the post-show conversion of your leads?
- the anticipated return on your investment?
- whether to rebook straight away, or wait?

What are the consequences of not measuring show performances?

Tradeshows: Optimizing and Measuring Performance—Key Learnings

1. Identify the most relevant tradeshows, conferences, and exhibitions or other events to reach your target audience.
2. Attract only qualified visitors in to your space or stand at these events.
3. Showcase your past and current success stories at all your events.
4. Staff your stands with experienced role-specific professionals.
5. Convert visitor requests for catalogs or brochures in to market intelligence gathering feedback.
6. Give qualified visitors a compelling reason to engage with you again.
7. Establish and measure your prospective ROI and ROOs from every event; draw objective conclusions for your future activity.

Case Study: CCS—South African Construction Computer Software in the UAE

Expectations

CCS wished to exploit the fast-growing construction market in the United Arab Emirates (UAE) by exhibiting at the Big 5 show in Dubai in 2013 over four days. They wanted to generate substantial sales from new customers and establish themselves as a respected and reliable provider of project control software, but could not afford a stand larger than 9m^2. Also, as a late entrant, they were located in a secondary position in the wrong hall.

Unforeseen Dangers

They ran the risk of being invisible among 5,500 exhibitors, being perceived as just another software provider and attracting the wrong prospects from the 60,000 visitors. The other danger was to spend too much time on demonstration of their software and failing to generate quality follow-up appointments leading to sales.

Outcomes

Figure 4.1 Engaging

By proactively approaching and qualifying passers-by consistently and relentlessly, they identified prospects who met their customer criteria. By restricting and obscuring access to their 3 × 3 m stand, they stimulated curiosity as to what was happening inside. By the use of trompe-l'oeil graphics, they created the 3D illusion of the interior of a plane. *Air stewardesses* delivered a themed overview of the company and case studies of their client successes. Seated *passengers* filled out *flight satisfaction surveys* to indicate their interest in a future software demonstration at CCS offices in Dubai.

Figure 4.2 Tiny stand, huge impact

This generated over 300 qualified leads, and nearly 50 requests for appointments. Furthermore, CCS enjoyed substantial publicity having attracted the attention of the organizers' PR company who promoted their stand online and in several publications.

Case Study: Howden Engineering Group (USA/UK) in India

Expectations

Howden, a global engineering manufacturer of a wide range of plant and equipment (industrial fans, compressors, and so on) wanted to grow their business in India and decided to exhibit at a tradeshow, Powergen in New Delhi 2009, over four days. They invested in a 6 × 6 m booth. The organizers had promised to deliver a substantial quantity of appropriate visitors.

Unforeseen Dangers

Having exhibited at previous Powergen shows in India without tangible success, Howden were concerned about committing resources to an event, which would once again yield little, if any, ROI. The involvement of a planning team, stand design, transport, and accommodation of personnel would divert attention, finances, and energy away from regular business.

Outcomes

A strategy was adopted incorporating a discreet space in which a version of an internationally televised gameshow experience (Mastermind) was delivered to engage visitors. Curiosity was generated outside the booth by large graphics featuring the iconic contestant's chair, unoccupied. Visitors were challenged to enter and take part. A proactive gameshow hostesses approached, qualified, and invited appropriate visitors in. The quiz delivered consistent Howden facts and case studies, in a light-hearted way, and stimulated enquiries for Howden's future involvement in Indian projects.

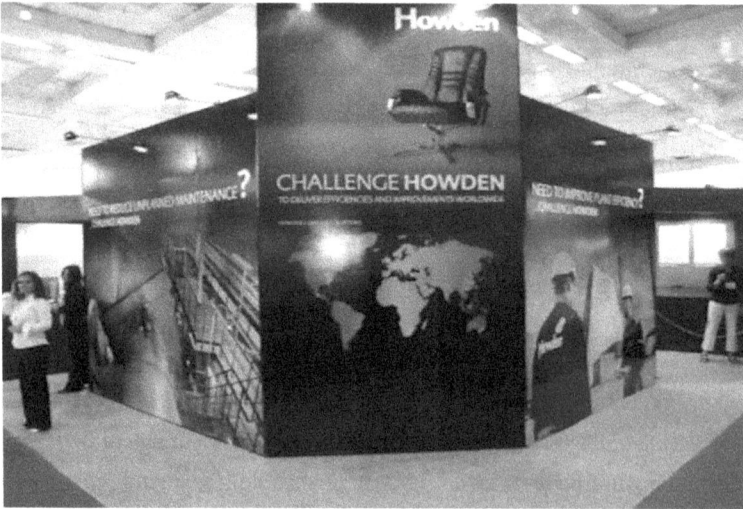

Figure 4.3 Howden's hidden challenge

Howden's key performance indicators (KPIs) for measuring the success of the show were all exceeded by more than 80 percent (over 250 requests for a future meeting). A model for future tradeshows was established. And, Howden's reluctance to exhibit was converted in to an active search for suitable events. They repeated their success in Germany at Powergen Europe one month later.

What actions should you take for your business?

Notes

_____

_____

_____

_____

_____

CHAPTER 5

B2B and D2C Options: Selecting Sales Channels

You have decided it is time for your business to consider exporting. Naturally, you would look for simplicity and minimal investment going forward. In considering the short- and long-term goals of your export initiative, your first thought may be that your current trading website will deliver sales from all over the world automatically and easily. You know of many would-be specialists offering a service to adapt, convert, update, or change your existing website into one that performs equally successfully in the international space. They promise outstanding results at a marginal cost and with minimal disruption.

Your next thought may be to appoint distributors. This is what your competitors are doing; this is the route that your industry traditionally takes; this can be seen as a logical extension to the way you do business in your home market. And, the main benefit is that it offers a single point of contact, a unique relationship to be developed. But, will your joint expectations and ambitions optimize and exploit the available market at a level that satisfies you both?

You need to clarify at the outset:

- who will control what: market intelligence, pricing, marketing, merchandising, communication, distribution, customer data, online presence, brand, fairs, events, sponsoring, advertising, exclusivity.
- who pays what costs: marketing, fairs, events, sponsorship, promotion, instore display, delivery, legal, training.
- what commitment do you expect: a contract, time, resources, territory, performance, exclusivity, range size, inventory holding,

new product development, terms and conditions, commissions, margins, discounts.

- how you will consistently measure progress and success.

There are many other channel options to consider: licensees, franchisees, joint ventures, key accounts, consignments, concessions, agents, own stores, subsidiaries, and so on. And today, you need to consider omni- or multichannel solutions to optimize your reach.

Whichever routes to market you choose, you will need a mutually acceptable and commercial contract to deal with all the aforementioned issues. By default, you will need to be compliant with local regulations. You also have to decide under which legislation and in what language(s) disputes are to be settled.

Business history is littered with companies and organizations that did not take enough time to commission a well thought out and binding contract for their relationship with channels or customers. Of course, the contract has to be realistic and proportionate to what is at stake. In an ideal world where your business relationship is flourishing, you may never have to take the contract out of your drawer, but it needs to be there for when you decide to review, renew, or relinquish a partnership, for whatever reason. A contract can rarely force a partner or channel to guarantee performance, but when it is well crafted, it will offer you the greatest protection.

One of the most contentious issues you will face from your channels may concern promotion: the advertising, social media, and brand presence of your products or services in their territory. There will be pressure on you to create and finance visibility. Your partners may well expect you to believe that without this profile success cannot be guaranteed. However, unless you have a global brand, throwing money at a high-profile campaign may be the least efficient strategy. Smart, highly targeted promotion emphasizing your unique selling proposition (USP) is far more likely to deliver the best returns.

(A)   Websites: Online *Brochure* and/or *Trading*

You have your own website, which you believe gives you credibility and visibility in your home market. You expect it to work whether it is a trading site or simply an online brochure, as well as whether you are selling products or services. You may have designed it as a simple information website describing the main activities of your company, introducing your key employees, and relating your history.

Maybe you feature your full product catalog in the hope that you will attract buyers. You might include blogs to create traction and engagement with readers. You obviously have a *contact us* section to capture the details of site visitors. You may even include customer comments, opinions, and endorsements.

Technically, you may have included password-protected access to different sections of the site to filter the availability of relevant information for different viewers with discrete requirements: typically end consumers or trade buyers, wholesalers or retailers, customers or prospects, those eligible for special offers or those who are not, and so on.

However, now you are contemplating turning what is essentially an information website, not only into a trading website, but one aimed at an international audience. You are solicited by third-party service providers who promise to convert your home market website into an international trading site with hardly any cost or input from you.

There is of course far more to this than meets the eye. Targeting, whether business-to-business (B2B) or direct-to-customer (D2C), currency, pricing structures and discounts, tariffs and value-added tax (VAT), language and imagery, layout and orientation, maintenance, staffing, payment methods, packaging, warehousing, and delivery, returns policy, and management are just some of the subjects that need to be addressed and resolved to make your site user-friendly for each territory or audience you wish to service.

Apart from selling via your own website hosted on your own platform, you may wish to offer your products and services via your own e-shop in externally hosted e-marketplaces, for example, Amazon, Alibaba, eBay, Zalando, Ozon, Allegro, Spartoo, Flipkart, Rakuten, and so on.

Ultimately, the most sensitive issue might be your pricing strategy. Every consumer, whether an individual or a business, needs to believe that they have bought from you at the best price and at the greatest value. Value originates from a combination of price, quality, and convenience of access.

If your business is discount-dependent, special care needs to be taken about the visibility of potentially conflicting offers in different countries. There may be the additional complication of multichannel supply with disparate prices due to the various cost structures associated with your choice of distribution channel, especially where there is the possibility of a buyer seeing many different prices for the same item.

Have you decided:

- which territories you wish to address?
- if you need a specific website for each territory?
- If you are selling B2B or D2C or B2B2C?
- open or password-protected access?
- who will create, design, maintain, and promote your different websites?
- who will *field* manage each territory?
- your multichannel pricing strategy?

How will you synchronize a multichannel strategy?

Obviously, you need to be visible to your audience(s). Herein lies the challenge. The World Wide Web is unmeasurable, almost limitless. How will the right people see your site? This is like finding a needle in a million bales of hay.

To make sure that you are constantly at the top of search engine lists, you need to own all the right key words. Not only do you need to own them, but you have to update their relevance, monitor their effectiveness, and manage their applicability in all the languages of your target territories. This of course requires investment in ads, search engine optimization (SEO), pay per click (PPC), banners, blogs, key opinion leaders (KOL), and the maintenance and control of your strategy and tactics to invite positive reaction from prospects and customers.

You have to be proactive in order to convert visitors into customers and customers into long-term clients. For this process to be successful, you will need to build and grow your own database to reach critical mass. It needs to be substantial, current, accurate, and compliant with the latest legislation, e.g., General Data Protection Regulation (GDPR) from the European Economic Community (EEC).

NB: The quality of a company's database has been proven to contribute considerably to the asset value of the entire business.

Have you strategized:

- your key word policy?
- your promotional campaigns?
- your database development?
- your social media?
- how your websites connect holistically with all your corporate marketing?
- the optimization and measurement of response and results?

What have you planned to do to internationalize your website?

(B)   Licensing

You are considering licensing. You may believe that you need less money to commercialize your products and services, bring your particular innovations to the target market more rapidly and open new opportunities at low cost. You expect to generate revenue more cost efficiently while still retaining ownership of your intellectual property (IP).

Your business owns IP, and you have the right to license it. Your brand, your production methods, your operating processes, your marketing techniques, and your business model ostensibly give you the option to consider appointing licensees anywhere in the world as long as your ownership of the IP is protected. You may consider recruiting licensees in certain territories. Perhaps, you are thinking of regions too remote or too small to supervise personally, or countries with a vastly different business culture to yours; or a market needing considerable product adaptation.

However, as with any successful partnership, the arrangement with your licensee(s) has to suit (be aligned with) all parties. For example: when your prospective licensee operates within a different business culture, you will need to judge whether any changes that they claim are necessary to your products, services, or processes are genuinely required for your success in that area or are actually requested in order to hijack them.

Have you agreed:

- the profile of your ideal licensee?
- how you will keep control over your invention or process?
- how you will monitor licensee compliance with your design policy, your product quality, your promotional style, your corporate brand image and values?
- who will own the rights to any new or improved products, services, or processes born from operating the license agreement?
- whose responsibility it is to monitor continuously any global and local competition?
- how you will deal with any lack of performance in commercializing the opportunity?
- what happens if the designated territory or region undergoes political or geological upheaval beyond the reasonable control of any party?

What is the cost to your future of signing a licensing agreement too hastily?

(C)   Franchising

You have a successful product, service, or process, *your brand*, and you may think you have a business model that can be replicated. So, you might consider offering franchises or dealerships to grow your own organization internationally … and fast. You believe you will not need to invest in distributors, agents, joint ventures, or subsidiaries.

If your proposition is proved as a commercial business model and it has enough appeal in your targeted territories, prospective franchisees (your future dive buddies) will be paying you operating fees and royalties. The upfront investment in infrastructure will be down to them: bricks and mortar, logistics, instore furniture, decor, point of sale, machinery, staffing, uniforms, and inventory. This represents a considerable commitment on their part. In the motor vehicle industry in particular, the dealership or franchise model is mainstream.

This attractive scenario requires you, by law in some territories, to be able to demonstrate a consistent business model yielding sustainable profits and proven growth over a minimum number of years.

Have you:

- tested whether your business model is truly portable?
- designed, written, and proved your business model?
- produced consistent profits and growth over a minimum number of years?
- launched, promoted, and exhibited your franchise opportunity?
- tested whether your business model is truly international?
- calculated what financing is required by your prospective franchisees?
- checked whether they are credit worthy?
- outsourced potential funding partners for your franchisees?
- built in the necessary controls of compliance with your corporate model, remotely?

What is involved in the preparation of your franchise model?

(D)   Joint Ventures or Partnerships

You believe that a joint venture or partnership may grow your business faster without the hazards of going it alone or acquiring another organization. You consider it a shortcut to exploiting and leveraging your particular IP before your competition moves in to a newly perceived niche or bags a particular contract or project. Perhaps, your proposed joint venture partner is in fact an existing distributor, or supplier, who also sees that this would make commercial sense. You expect to reduce the barriers to market entry, share the talent of each other's staff, benefit from each other's patents or licenses, and of course, share costs, risks, and profits.

For the sake of clarification, a joint venture or a partnership starts with different individuals or companies coming together in the pursuit of a common objective. In the interests of simplicity, the parties decide to work together via their existing companies, without the need to create a new entity. This is either a loose arrangement unencumbered by a legal agreement between the parties, a partnership, which can be clarified through a written agreement, or an *unincorporated joint venture*.

In other cases, the parties create a new independent company, an *incorporated joint venture*, with specific projects in mind, agreed expectations, and compatible methods of working. The reality of an incorporated joint venture is that you would be running a company with individuals with whom you may or may not have done business previously. You would both expect to enjoy the benefits of this arrangement equally.

You would need to agree in advance whether your relationship with your proposed partner will have a finite time period ending on a predetermined date or if it is intended to be an ongoing partnership.

Have you reflected on:

- whether you would prefer an incorporated or unincorporated joint venture?
- how aligned your expectations are: financial and other?
- how you will resolve issues of differences in cultures, languages, and values?
- whether you both have the necessary commercial and personal chemistry, communication skills and energy to drive the partnership to success?
- how you will report and make the best tactical decisions?
- Assuming potentially unlimited liability for the actions of the other party?
- Your shared vision of success, how and when you will exit profitably?

How damaging could an ill-conceived partnership or joint venture be?

(E)   Distributors

You may be naturally drawn to appointing distributors as your principal channels because they are arguably perceived on the surface to be the cheapest and easiest route to your uncharted territories. You consider recruiting a distributor on the basis of their known access to these markets, and the fact that they have an existing organization with a solid reputation. You assume that they will undertake most of the required investment because you are offering them generous trading discounts.

A distributorship is basically another business like yours. They have similar core behaviors, expectations, and challenges. Nevertheless, the distributor margin imposes an extra cost layer on your products or services. The reality is that distributors need to earn enough to cover their own commercial structure such as offices, sales teams, showroom, warehouse, online sales function, and so on, and they need to make a respectable profit.

However, there may be valuable major accounts in the territory that you would wish to target and which you may be prevented from accessing via your distributor because of the various layers of profit margin required by all parties.

Distributors will usually have a portfolio of other brands and products complementary to yours, which is why you may be considering appointing them in the first place. Naturally, your chosen distributor needs to be enthusiastic about your products and services and see where they fit in to their overall offering.

This brings up the inevitable dilemma of providing samples. Your distributors may well expect samples of your complete range on the basis of *no samples, no sales*. Even when they are prepared to pay for them, if your samples are limited, you will have to manage distributors' expectations stringently from the outset.

Remember also that your distributors will own your customers. They will be taking the orders, buying the inventory, servicing consumers, collecting payments, and will be totally responsible for paying you. In the interests of a distributor's self-preservation, your access to genuine real-time market intelligence, product feedback, trends, knowledge of customers' profiles, contact details, preferences, competitors, and hidden opportunities may be denied to you or at best distorted.

In some territories, distributors may not exist or will be limited. There may be very few prospects who could agree to be your distributors in underdeveloped countries, such as Africa, or where the cultural or political environment has not previously allowed the growth of private businesses, such as China or Russia, or where the population is too small, such as Iceland or Fiji.

In the final analysis, where your expectations of a distributor's investment and involvement do not match theirs, they may feel marginalized and not fully honor what you understand has been agreed between you.

Have you articulated:

- your ambitions for the territory and ascertained those of your intended distributor?
- your expectations of where your distributor must operate and perform?
- your expectations of where your products will rank within your distributor's current range and brand offering?
- which of their current lines or brands may clash with yours?
- your samples policy?
- what the agreed process is for dealing with discrepancies in deliveries?
- how the parties will deal with major accounts who require substantial terms and discounts?
- how you will optimize, control, and validate your distributors' performance?
- how you will terminate a distributorship when necessary and deal with outstanding debts, inventory, retention of customers, and so on?

What is at stake if you recruit the wrong distributor(s)?

(F)   Sales Agents

When you are considering the key elements of cost, control, and commitment, with regard to your customer base and your pricing strategy, commission-only agents may appear to be your perfect channel. After all, sales agents only earn revenue when they sell your products and services and payment is received. Usually, agents prefer the independence of running their own show, without having to report to corporate management. Your expectations of an agent may be almost as high as those of a distributor. Indeed, they will know the market and probably have a portfolio of complementary products or services. They should be able to deliver sales quickly.

It should be noted that to all intents and purposes, an agent is your *de facto* representative in the territory. Any promises they make to your customers are potentially binding on you and may expose you to the consequences of nonperformance. Induction and training, together with a clear and detailed understanding of your products, services, and terms, is essential. In any contract between you and your agents, you need to be specific about what they are authorized to promise.

As with distributors, the commission-only agency concept may not exist, or there may be too few to select from to service your chosen territory. On the other hand, in certain cultures and countries, for example, the United States, the commission-only agent is by far the most common form of sales force because of its flexibility and the ease of hiring and firing, which is not always the case in Europe.

In an agency relationship, you will be invoicing customers directly. After all, they are contracted to your company, not to your agent. So, there needs to be clarity about who is responsible for servicing them, for example, dealing with translation and communication; short, late, incorrect, or substandard deliveries; adding or amending orders; delivery dates and locations; special enquiries; and so on.

The allocation of product samples (as for distributors), that is, who gets what, how many, whether they are paid for or not becomes a strategic consideration in terms of potential return on this considerable investment.

Once again, in the case of unsatisfactory performance, you have to decide whether to replace your agent, or if it is more beneficial to try to remedy any shortcomings. Your investment in recruiting and training an agent, as well as the time and invisible costs associated with this process, need to be evaluated carefully.

Remember your agent is your partner. You are interdependent.

Have you worked out:
- what type of sales agent suits you, for example, what complementary products or services they carry and with what brand profile?
- what agency model works best in your chosen territory, for example, sole agent, general agent, exclusive agent?
- if it is the responsibility of the territory or general agent to recruit sub-agents?
- who funds induction and training, showrooms, promotion, literature, translation, and so on?
- your samples policy?
- who funds, controls, and promotes regional, national, and international trade fairs?
- how you will validate new accounts and unusual orders?
- commission levels—taking in to account special customer terms and conditions?
- when you remit commission to your sales agents: at the point of order, complete and correct delivery, or cleared payment?
- what is the agreed process for dealing with discrepancies?
- who validates customer credit worthiness and who chases bad debts?
- how you will nurture, develop, motivate, and monitor your agents effectively?
- how you will terminate an agency when necessary with regard to outstanding debts, inventory, retention of customers, and so on?

What is at stake when you recruit the wrong agent?

(G)   Consignments

Your sales teams have started to knock on doors in your target territory, but your products or services are failing to generate immediate interest. This may be because your brand is unknown; there are well-established products or services already in the marketplace, which are perceived to be similar to yours; instore floor and shelf space is already under pressure;

you have no history of demonstrating the added value of your products or services in this territory. When a territory or account is strategically important to your export ambitions, you may, as a last resort, want to consider the sale or return (SOR) or consignment model because you believe that you will penetrate the market more swiftly than in any other way.

SOR or consignment selling means that you will be sending your valuable inventory at your cost to an outlet where you have little control over the sales, marketing, merchandising, staff, storage conditions, or inventory (e.g., where *leakage* or theft is prevalent). You could be driving blind with inadequate support.

You need to make sure that you have effective monitoring and measurement systems in place, that you have calculated the right product range, enough inventory, and ability to replenish your best-selling lines in order to exploit fully the underlying demand.

This type of selling is often temporarily deployed as a forerunner to appointing outlets reluctant to carry your products or services when their performance or appeal is as yet unproven in the marketplace.

Have you taken in to account:

- what measurement and monitoring system you will apply?
- what to do with unpacked, visibly priced, or damaged inventory at the end of a campaign?
- how you will recondition goods to make them saleable elsewhere?
- the cost of clearing surplus and non-current inventory, from multiple locations?
- how scalable and sustainable this business model is?

How do you control the profitability of your consignment business?

(H) Major Accounts

Attracting major accounts is the aspiration of many product manufacturers or service providers. You may believe that it will be a simpler and more cost-effective route to your ultimate customers. You would enjoy wide distribution, volume orders, high-profile exposure, instore presence, endorsement, advertising, single-source invoicing and payment, and often a single delivery point.

Naturally, you will need to discover whether enough key accounts exist in your chosen territory in sufficient numbers to build your brand and sell consistently increasing volumes or not, especially in markets with a history of limited mass retailing or trading, for example, Russia, China, third-world developed countries, and so on.

Where effective key accounts do exist, you are more than likely to be aiming at a mature, crowded marketplace. Your real challenge will be access, in a notably risk-averse culture and sector, and ultimately profitability, especially when buyers expect to call the shots about every aspect of your presence in their outlets.

This approach comes at a price. Each major account will represent a significant proportion of your sales at compressed margins. You may have to survive in demanding and turbulent conditions requiring special resources, for example, white label ranges, customized products or services, terms and conditions, and so on, which could compromise your long-term presence.

Have you answered:

- why a potential key account might take your products or services in the first place?
- what guarantee you offer that your product will sell, profitably?
- whether you can afford their credit terms: are you a manufacturer or a banker?
- if you are able to supply any special or own branded products or services in the volumes that they may require?
- what you will do with products ordered, manufactured, packed, but not called off?
- whether you can meet their contractual terms and afford any non-performance penalties, for example, deliveries?
- what happens to faulty, damaged, and unsold inventory?

- whether you will earn enough margin to survive and grow?
- how exposed you will be to any individual account?

How sustainable are major accounts?

(I)   Concessions

You are confident that the appeal of your products or service will be strong in your targeted territory. All you need is customer traffic, of the right quality and quantity. You may have identified retail outlets, shopping malls, department stores, cruise ships, airport duty-free areas, or other high-traffic locations. You still prefer to control the merchandising, inventory levels, pricing, and staff to represent your brand consistently. *Shop in shop* commission-only concessions could be the answer.

Your brands may be unknown in the area. Perhaps, your targeted outlets are unsure that your range will deliver enough growth and profit opportunity and will strategically complement what they already carry. When a retailer prefers not to resell your products or services, allocate shelf or floor space, or indeed buy inventory at their cost for whatever reason, they may be more open to the concession model. This applies also when you anticipate that a larger instore presence would deliver significantly higher returns, but the retailer is not prepared to commit the outlay.

A concession removes the greatest part of a retailer's outlay and risk. You provide the inventory, you bring a proven merchandising style, you train the floor sales staff (unmanned concession) and may even decide to install your own team (manned concession). Your contract with the outlet owners will require you to pay agreed commissions on goods or services sold. There may be other obligations to be agreed by each party, for example, concerning minimum opening hours, inventory storage, movement, and supply, cash handling, and so on. The challenge is to control the operation securely and systematically from any distance in order to avoid leakage and damage to your brand profile.

You need to be convinced that the site, your location within the outlet, the customer traffic and quality, the accessibility and opening hours, the health and safety supervision, the proximity to complementary products or services all justify your presence.

Are you happy with:

- the quantity, quality, and regularity of the anticipated traffic?
- the control you have over where you are sited within the retail space?
- your host retailer's sensitivity and response to changes in shopping behavior, for example, online business, click-and-collect, seasonal travel, trends, ethical issues?
- your staffing options (unmanned or manned) how you will recruit, train, motivate, and monitor the attendance and performance of the sales team remotely?
- your capacity to gather reliable market intelligence and customer feedback?
- your ability to service and manage your concessions, for example, through your own local warehouse, third-party logistics partner, direct delivery, local production?
- your control over sales, inventory movement, replenishment, clearance of slow-moving lines, security, and leakage?
- the levels of commission you have contracted to pay, especially in the case of promotions and clearance sales?
- when and how you are paid?
- the flexibility you have to expand easily following success?
- the ongoing financial stability and viability of your host outlet?

How viable is your concession business model?

(J)   Outlets or Own Stores

You are already operating successful stores or outlets in your home market. You recognize that serious customers want to see, touch, try before they buy a product. You understand the mechanics that allow your goods to sell at the right time, at the right price. You have a proven concept that delivers consistently profitable returns within your own bricks-and-mortar proposition. Instinctively, you are tempted to replicate the success of your stores abroad.

From your knowledge of how your traditional consumers behave in your home market, you have developed the most attractive instore, multisensory environment, for example, via store fittings, lighting, appropriate music and scent, audio-visual interactivity along a controlled customer journey, a theater of emotional impact on the mood of your audience, the retail experience. Once you have validated your product or service selection, you need to research and test whether and how your version will work in your targeted countries and what changes have to be made when you are operating in unfamiliar territories.

You also need to respond to local culture in order to create a dynamic and effective series of instore and external promotional events spread over the calendar year, synchronized with local bank holidays, anniversaries, school holidays, sport, cultural, religious or commercial festivals, for example, Christmas, Diwali, Ramadan, Chanukah, Chinese New Year, Valentine, Easter, Halloween, Mother's Day, Father's Day, Black Friday, Thanksgiving, and so on.

Your strategy regarding the location of your store needs thorough scrutiny, given the intense pressure on instore high-street retailing currently being experienced globally. Wherever you are looking to site your outlet, online purchasing is reducing customer traffic. Your online trading offer has to echo the instore experience to the greatest possible extent. Today, ease of transaction and collection is paramount, whether instore or online, and has to adapt to local buying behavior and shopping trends.

Have you resolved that:

- your concept appeals emotionally and culturally to your new customers?
- your customers will be able to read, understand, and connect with your brand proposition?
- your new customers will react, behave, and navigate your floor space so that they know how to find what they are looking for?
- customer service expectations are the same as in your home market?

- your communications and promotional campaigns are adaptable to engage locals effectively, are customer-friendly, and politically correct?
- you have contained any financial commitments (rents, leases, taxes, utilities, staff, logistics, and so on) to a predetermined duration, with clear options?
- a termination of contractual commitments is possible for whatever reason with limited and affordable penalties?
- you have the flexibility to expand easily following success?
- you can afford the write-off of inventory, fixtures, fittings, and so on in the event of closure?

What is your total exposure when opening your own stores?

(K)   Subsidiaries

You have tried some or all of the aforementioned channels, but with limited success. You are not satisfied with the current performance and direction of your export business via, for example, your stores, your key accounts, or your concessions or consignments. You conclude that your remoteness from day-to-day control is hampering your results. You have identified that the missing component is your own local hands-on senior management trained by you and directly accountable to you. You have decided to recruit a key individual to open your subsidiary in the strategically targeted territory. You are convinced that this region can sustain its own sales, marketing and customer service team, office, workshop, and showroom. You believe that the answer lies in local management and staff with existing knowledge of the territory, local languages, and business culture and will deliver instant access to the market.

The recruitment, training, and induction of the executive, who will become your strategic appointment, are crucial for your success. All subsequent staff engagements flow from his or her talents and depend on his or her leadership.

Although of lesser significance to the hiring of an effective territory executive, your commitment to premises may also tie you up for an indeterminate length of time, with stringent exit terms and conditions.

If you decide after a trial period that you need to abandon that particular region because it is still not performing according to expectations or indeed to expand because it is now working well, you have to allow for the coordination of your progress within your contractual commitments. Otherwise, you may be faced with considerable penalties. It is imperative that from the outset any negotiation with landlords, contractors, service providers, and so on incorporate as much flexibility to reduce or expand your operations within a realistic time frame.

Have you thought about:

- what strategy you will use to recruit the right senior manager: agency, direct advertising, business contacts, customers' or competitors' staff, head hunter, social media, and so on?
- agency fees, guarantees, and accountability, what happens if the recruitment fails, and how long it will take before you conclude that it is not working?
- what ill-will you could suffer following termination of contracts with existing channels, for example, distributors, agents who may want to spike your new initiative?
- how you will ensure that staff feel part of your company, adopt your culture and values, despite operating at arm's length?
- what additional office or warehouse or logistic overheads you will incur in connection with rents, leases, utilities, inventory, fixtures, and fittings?
- whether a termination of your contractual commitments is possible for whatever reason with limited and affordable penalties, if necessary?
- you have the flexibility to expand easily following success?
- the write-off of inventory, fixtures, fittings, and so on in the event of closure?

What are the hidden costs of a dysfunctional subsidiary?

(L) Acquisitions

You believe that a shortcut to accessing a new market quickly is to buy an already established local business or brand that is similar or complementary to yours. You can afford to fund this potentially more direct and efficient route. You have identified a suitable target. You may know their management and modus operandi. They may be a current customer, supplier, or competitor, and this seems to offer an instant readymade profit stream.

Given that any acquisition, even within your own country, is fraught with hurdles, a foreign purchase brings with it many extra challenges: the ongoing involvement of the owners, effective due diligence, taxation, legislation, accounting, and financial procedures, all conducted in a foreign language within a different culture. And of course, the key issue is agreeing a realistic valuation of the assets and the ongoing viability. In some countries, you may even be obliged to have a local partner in order to own a local business.

Business is about reducing risk and maximizing returns. Buying another business is possibly the greatest gamble you will make. While the valuation process of the acquisition is in itself highly subjective, depending on how much you are ready to pay against what they are prepared to accept, you may have to commit significant funds upfront in the discovery process. For safety, you will need specialist advice throughout. And, you will need to retain the ongoing services of key personnel in the interests of continuity. Paramount in this decision is the measurement of what adverse impact the project will have on the smooth running of your existing business.

Have you drilled down to:

- whether the communication between all parties is effective, open, and honest? Does yes mean yes?
- how you will purchase the business as safely as possible? Everything upfront? Staged payments? Payments on performance, and so on?
- whether your funding of the acquisition will dilute your equity in your own company and threaten your future?

- what the impact of absorbing a completely foreign entity with its own business culture will be on your organization, especially on your people?
- what you will do with existing brand or product names? Change, remove, adapt, or leave as they are?
- how you will integrate unfamiliar or incompatible operating systems, people, and processes?
- what budget you will allocate to deal adequately with any contingencies?
- when realistically you can expect a respectable return on investment?

What is your total exposure in gambling on a foreign acquisition?

B2B and D2C Options: Selecting Sales Channels—Key Learnings

1. Consider a single channel or multichannel strategy for each territory or situation.
2. Conduct thorough due diligence into who you are intending to deal with.
3. Negotiate and agree commercial contracts or arrangements that are mutually beneficial and allow attractive profit margins for all channel partners.
4. Clarify thoroughly who owns responsibility for each function and process within the partnership; agree which channel partner pays for what.
5. Invest the time and care to develop chemistry toward mutually rewarding commercial relationships. Always remember you are a partner to your customers and your suppliers are partners to you.
6. Measure ongoing success to determine whether your partnership is failing, succeeding, or has been outgrown.
7. Always have a prepared exit or future strategy anticipating any potential costs in case of failure or success beyond expectations.

Case Study: Retailing in South Korea

Expectations

Serious would-be exporters will undoubtedly consider exploiting the potential of South Korea. The expectations of those who have entered this market are driven by the appeal of a highly developed country, a population of over 50 million, the world's 11th largest economy by nominal gross domestic product (GDP) and the 8th largest importer (at the time of writing this book). Its retail sector is acknowledged to be fast paced, a quick adopter of change and innovation, growing dynamically online and via convenience stores.

Unforeseen Dangers

The growth of the South Korean economy has slowed recently, resulting in consumers becoming highly price conscious. They are buying cheaper products online and also tending to buy food from convenience stores as opposed to eating in restaurants or bars. Domestic retail conglomerates, like Lotte, Hyundai, Shinsegae, and so on, are inundating the local market via their multiple retail outlets. Homegrown start-up online suppliers such as WeMakePrice, TMON, and Coupang have become major players. Also, to assume that Korean customers would accept products imported from the West takes no account of their demanding expectations and refined tastes.

Any manufacturer eyeing the Korean market needs to understand in depth the unique nature and character of Korean culture.

Outcomes

Different companies have taken different routes to the market in South Korea:

Carrefour, a French multinational hypermarket chain, decided to enter the Korean market via their own subsidiary. While their big-box concept had proved so far to be an internationally successful model, their universal operating standards did not satisfy Korean consumer demands. Details such as store layout, shelf height, package sizing, fresh food selection, and customer service all missed the mark. Added to this, the language barrier and the employment of French managers who were unable to handle vast cultural differences contributed to a disconnect with their own staff and their customers. This led ultimately to failure and their abandoning South Korea.

The case of Carrefour is not unique. Other multinational retailers met the same fate for similar reasons.

IKEA, however, a Swedish multinational retailer of affordable self-assembly home furniture, also entered the Korean market by establishing a wholly owned subsidiary. They were successful largely because of their competitive pricing combined with their unique global business model.

Costco, an American multinational operating via a chain of membership-only warehouses, and the second largest retailer in the world, entered the Korean market through a strategy of forming a joint venture with a local major retailer. Eventually, their success enabled them to buy out their joint venture partner.

Other successful foreign retailers, like Boots and 7/11, who partnered with local conglomerates have survived and grown in South Korea by appreciating local culture and satisfying customer preferences in far greater depth.

Case Study: UK Children's Buggy Brand Cosatto in China

Expectations:

A persistent Chinese ex-supplier to children's buggy designer Cosatto pleaded to distribute the brand in China. Collaboration with this former supplier had previously been terminated due to a clash of personalities and the unreliability of their product quality. A distributor relationship was discussed during a hurried conversation in a coffee shop at Shanghai airport. A 250k-pound order was unexpectedly waiting for Cosatto's owner when he arrived back at his UK office. There was no financial risk owing to a 30 percent upfront deposit to start production in China and the balance to be paid free on board (FOB) before shipping inland. This arrangement lasted 2.5 years and generated about 3M-pound worth of turnover. Cash was positive, margins generous, without serious price negotiation or product adjustments for the market. Expectations of future business growth were high.

Unforeseen Dangers

Deposit payments became progressively delayed. The outstanding amounts due before shipping also slowed down, leaving finished production awaiting delivery and occupying valuable factory floor space. Frustration set in. A surprise e-mail from the supplier's wife informed Cosatto that her husband had been arrested. His ensuing detention lasted for two years, and a clear explanation of the causes never reached Cosatto. Business dropped away abruptly. And, during the investigation, Cosatto's owner was questioned about possible involvement in the fraud. He was afraid to go back to China and being jailed.

Outcomes

Cosatto's owner was eventually cleared of any involvement. It was discovered that there were two sizable lots of inventory in China, one ostensibly in the hands of the jailed distributor's own business partners and one in the hands of his wife. The goods had all been paid for but not sold out. A new distributor expressed interest to Cosatto in taking on the brand, but he was concerned about the volume of goods being cleared at low prices to liquidate the remaining inventory. While the new distributor appeared to be credible, Cosatto's presence in China was suffering from the resulting damage to their brand. It would take an estimated three to four years to recover the lost business. While there had been an exciting opportunity for Cosatto to enter the Chinese market early and become a major player, the buggy market had moved on and become fiercely competitive due to ambitious new entrants.

Case study courtesy of Andrew Kluge, CEO, Cosatto

What actions should you take for your business?

Notes

_____

_____

_____

_____

_____

CHAPTER 6

Cashflow: Balancing Prudence and Growth

You are managing your existing cashflow efficiently. You believe that your foreign customers have respect for prompt payment according to the terms and conditions you have agreed. You expect that once an order has been placed and delivered, the cash will flow in.

"Turnover is vanity, profit is sanity … but cash is king."

While any order is usually considered fulfilled when it is delivered and paid for, international transactions will necessitate much more third-party involvement to bring in your cash.

While your cashflow may run satisfactorily in your existing business, it does not mean that this will be the case when you export. You will need to operate your transactions in accordance with a plethora of acronyms and jargon relating to international commerce: IBAN (International Bank Account Number), BIC (Bank Identifier Code), SWIFT (Society for Worldwide Interbank Financial Telecommunication, Bank transfer), L/C (Letter of Credit), ICLC (Irrevocable and Confirmed Letter of Credit), FOB/CIF (Free on Board/Cost Insurance Freight), Incoterms 2000 (International Commercial Terms), BL (Bill of Lading), BE (bill of exchange), FB (currency Forward Booking), and so on. You will have to become familiar with and understand all of the above.

You will depend to a great extent on service providers whom you may never have used or heard of before: freight forwarders, currency forward-booking agents, value-added tax (VAT) representatives, processing or warehousing or logistics companies, international banks and insurers, third-party provider (TP), and so on. Each of these parties adds to your costs and reduces your margin unless you can raise your prices to cover them.

Your payment terms have to take in to account some or all of the above extra fees and have to be identified, clarified, and negotiated in any export deal. Negotiating terms and conditions invariably highlights the topic of your prospect's ability and attitude toward payment. Successful long-term business is built on sustainable relationships, rather than individual transactions. Your aim going forward should be to develop a healthy relationship while regularly attending to the sensitive issues of credit worthiness, payment history, outstanding debt, delivery, quality shortcomings, and so on in a positive, constructive, and agreeable framework … without drama. You need to ensure that your business can recover safely in the event of an emergency.

Can your business afford to be paid late, or never?

(A)   Credit Control

Unexpectedly, you receive an order from an unknown customer. It may have come through a third-party referral, or from a trade show introduction, or from a random source. In any event, you are hungry for the business and delighted at the prospect of a new customer, especially if the order is of high value. You are tempted to take the order, as it will accelerate the achievement of your sales targets; it may open a new market; it will motivate your teams; it will enhance your brand recognition and exposure.

Alongside their order, the prospects may have requested samples to benchmark them against the delivery to follow. Providing samples before taking an order is a sensitive issue, especially if there is no history with the prospect. Samples may be costly to produce in short runs, and once they are delivered, you run the risk of giving unscrupulous customers the opportunity to source elsewhere or directly copy your designs.

Beyond the honest aim of growing your business through opportunities that appear from *good fortune*, there are today highly sophisticated professional cyber fraudsters. Examples of theft by entities or individuals appearing to be legitimate are widespread and increasing exponentially. Passwords, e-mail addresses, and security codes are anything but safe. Serious criminals have developed seemingly innocuous ways of acquiring them by inviting a business to react to what appears to be a genuine inquiry from somebody you know. When something feels wrong, it often is. And, every possible firewall and common-sense approach needs to be deployed.

What due diligence will you conduct around:

- the prospect's true identity. Are they a registered company? And, who ultimately owns the business? Are they legitimate, a competitor, or a rogue business in disguise?
- what size they are: turnover, employees, profits, assets, and so on?
- what their credit rating is, and how long they have been operating?
- the quality and credibility of the prospect's website and their current product offering?
- identifying the industries, territories, niches, quality, and price points in which they operate?
- how you will authenticate whether it is a one-off order or the genuine initiation of significant new regular business?
- whether they expect samples and how you will protect yourself from potential copying?
- the extent to which this unexpected order will interfere with your regular production?
- the impact on your service to your regular customers?

What are the risks of not thoroughly researching prospects?

(B)   Incoterms

You may expect that the tried-and-tested logistics that work within your home markets will operate smoothly abroad. They have been cost efficient, reliable, and punctual. And, you and your teams are used to the paperwork.

In reality, even a local delivery can be a challenge, and now, your products or services need to reach your customer at a more remote location. The further distant your delivery point is, the more vulnerable and exposed you will be to unforeseen factors such as geology, the

weather, and manmade obstacles, which are more likely to disrupt a usually familiar operation. These conditions are often beyond your control,
for example, hurricane, earthquake, flooding, political turmoil, security
challenges, industrial unrest, changing tariffs, and legislation, terrorism,
drones, theft, hijacking, and so on. They are all unpredictable and significant barriers to a reliable delivery process.

To monitor the movement of goods, there are various systems and
processes in place. International delivery terms are structured via *Incoterms* (International Commercial Terms), which are set by the International Chamber of Commerce (ICC), to clarify who is responsible for
which stage of the process. They take account of international commercial law and are widely used by the export community. Incoterms 2010
include 11 rules, each of which is denominated by a combination of
three letters. Each rule corresponds to predefined commercial terms that
explain for each party the tasks, costs, and risks associated with the international transportation of goods, for example, FOB, CIF, DDP (Delivered Duty Paid), EXW (EX Works), and so on. An incoterm is not a
legally binding commitment on its own and should be part of a more
comprehensive sales contract incorporating, for example, insurance cover,
payment terms, packaging, and the choice of currency.

Payments are usually made during and/or after the delivery process,
that is, when goods or services have finally reached customers, which
match their expectations. Of course, there may be circumstances in
which a new prospect has agreed to pay a pre-production deposit. Payment upfront may be required when there is a doubt about their credit
worthiness. The task of managing the synchronization of payments
with the various stages of delivery is in itself a crucial factor in developing and maintaining your ongoing relationship with new and existing
customers.

Have you clearly established:

- what contractual delivery terms have been agreed between
  seller and buyer?
- at what stage your responsibility for the delivery begins and
  when it is transferred to the customer and which incoterm?

- who is responsible for any damage incurred from the time the goods leave your premises to the time they reach your customer?
- what happens when goods are held up in customs for any reason, and how this situation will affect payments?
- what insurance you need to cover your delivery?
- *Retention of Title:* who owns the goods at what stage of the delivery process?

Who pays the price for ambiguous delivery terms?

(C)   Insurance

You have been sold a policy by a well-established international credit insurance company with a convincing proposition. You may have been introduced to the insurers via your membership of a trade or professional body. You are reassured by the knowledge that other companies in your sector use them as well.

You now receive a significant order from a new foreign prospect. You are bound to offer credit terms to close the deal. Inevitably, you need to consider what happens if you do not get paid. You will also have to consider what happens when you have shipped an order and your client claims that it is faulty, incomplete, incorrect, or late, and a dispute ensues . . .

Insurance companies by definition cover what they perceive to be low risk at the time you sign your policy contract. They may from time to time also send updates to your cover on current accounts that, unknown to you, have become financially unsound. In these cases, your cover may cease with immediate effect. Insurers may also withhold cover in a region or country where the political or economic situation has become uncertain for a time, for example, Greece, Ukraine, Russia, Iran.

If you wish to protect your debts and recoup the cost of insuring, you may decide to add a surcharge to your invoices or build the cost in to your pricing and allocate the proceeds to your own *insurance fund* effectively self-insuring. When your credit control department is doing its job efficiently, you may reflect on whether you need a policy at all.

To insure or not to insure, that is the question . . .

In which case, what:

- happens if your customer refuses to pay for whatever reason?
- is your policy excess?
- does your policy exclude?
- happens when cover for a territory where you have reliable customers is withdrawn?
- happens if you are notified of a customer's insolvency when their order is being produced or is ready for shipping?
- do you say to a customer when your agreed payment terms need to be revisited because of your insurers?
- does the *small print* say?

How do you measure the true value of insurance?

(D)   Currency

You are trading successfully in your own marketplace in your own currency. You assume, therefore, that currency will be the least of your problems and your export prospects will be happy to trade in yours.

Unless you have a uniquely desirable product, it is actually unlikely that your target customers will be happy to trade in your currency, especially online. They may not have the facilities to transfer money abroad easily. Whether paying you by bank transfer or credit card or some other method, your customers will be faced with exchange rates and foreign transfer fees, which may deter them from dealing with you.

Alternatively, you may decide to price your products in your prospects' currency. However, when you calculate their prices, you will need to anticipate the time lapses between the conversion of your standard prices into their currency, the quotation to your customers, the receipt and confirmation of their order, its delivery and invoicing as well as the moment when the payment actually lands in your bank account.

You ignore the impact of international currency management at your peril. All currencies are volatile to different degrees and their movement is an unknown risk to your business. Exchange rate management is in itself a minefield and may benefit from professional input.

You may consider opening your own foreign bank account to facilitate transactions. Although it looks to be a logical and simple option, this procedure has its own complications and pitfalls and is usually more hazardous than the banks imply in their promotional material.

Have you weighed up:

- whether to transact your business in your currency, that of your prospects, or a third option?
- whether your prospects would deal with you in your currency, and would this limit the business they can give you?
- what extra cost foreign currency transactions will add, at both ends?
- who pays which fees and how they will affect your margins?
- how to protect yourself against abnormal adverse currency fluctuations affordably?
- how and when you will buy your foreign currency and at what exchange rate you will trade?
- if foreign banks would be willing to open an account if you have no trading history in their territory?
- even if they are … how long they will take and how much it will cost?

How will you mitigate the impact of exchange rate fluctuation?

(E)   Payment

You have taken an order from an export customer. You are excited and optimistic about this promising relationship and its potential for your company. All you have to do now is make sure that you are paid fully … on time … without complication. You want your money as soon as possible. Your customer wants to pay as late as possible and, of course, *cash is king*.

Inevitably, the desirability of your brand, your products, or your services will influence the payment terms to be agreed. On a scale of options, if your proposition is strong, you may be able to demand upfront payment. However, if your customer is dominant, and you want their business, you may be expected to grant extended credit terms.

Upfront payment before the goods or services are delivered appears at first sight to be by far the safest way of being paid. This approach, however, demonstrates the lowest level of trust in the potential of your future business relationship. Remember: as you are dependent on your customers to pay you for your goods or services *fully and on time*, you are inevitably at the mercy of what they sell and how they are performing overall as a business . . .

You may decide to offer extended credit terms to demonstrate a higher degree of confidence in your client. Deciding on a strategy for your credit terms policy requires you to balance the risk of not being paid against the future growth of your export business.

International payment tools, which incorporate any element of credit and payment guarantee, typically demand that the full settlement amount should be available immediately and deposited in a bank account. From the buyer's point of view, this is equivalent to an upfront payment. As the seller, you do not have access to your money until completion of the transaction. This applies to an Irrevocable and Confirmed Letter of Credit (ICLC) which the buyer must open and pay for. To do so, the bank issuing the ICLC will only release the funds when the agreed terms and conditions have been satisfied. The same conditions apply to bank guarantees, which all come at a cost.

There may be occasions when one of your accounts is in difficulty or even on the verge of insolvency, irrespective of whether this comes as a surprise or they have given you warning. They may still have payments outstanding as well as confirmed orders in production. You stand to incur substantial losses. On the one hand, they may offer you nothing, but on the other hand, subject to the quality of your business relationship, they may present you with a credible business recovery plan and ask you for extended payment terms and inventory support.

Have you estimated:

- what your customer's long-term aspirations for your commercial relationship are?
- what terms you can afford to agree to stimulate the maximum amount of business safely?
- when upfront payment is necessary in your ascent toward a more flexible arrangement later?
- what terms your competitors are offering for similar products or services, whether and to what extent you need to match or improve on them?

- what facilities and systems you have in place to ensure that international payments are made in accordance with your agreed terms, and you remain a respected creditor?
- what to do if your customer no longer wants to receive and pay for goods already produced, in spite of your contractually agreed delivery and payment terms?
- what to do in the case of a customer's insolvency? Collaborate in a recovery plan or write it off?

How much growth will you sacrifice through shortsighted payment terms?

Cashflow: Balancing Prudence and Growth—Key Learnings

1. Be constantly aware of prevailing international exchange rate fluctuations . . . forward book currency whenever appropriate.
2. Agree delivery terms between parties for each order, taking into consideration *Retention of Title*.
3. When negotiating payment terms with strategic partners bear in mind your long-term relationship.
4. To mitigate your exposure, use affordable insurance or secured payment tools where appropriate.
5. Establish and maintain robust credit control processes to ensure prompt payment. Train your staff to enforce agreed payment terms in a professional way.
6. Always have a *Plan B* in the case of possible customer payment default.
7. Cash is king.

Case Study: B2C Payment in China

Expectations

Any exporting company wishing to sell directly to customers in China (e.g., via a wholly owned subsidiary) will be aiming to benefit from the huge population, their thirst for *Western* consumer goods and the ongoing growth of the domestic market. Product sales may take place through retail or online shops, or services, via for example, restaurants, fast food, health and sports clubs. Exporters may anticipate that payments are transacted in ways similar to those in the West.

Unforeseen Dangers

By far the greatest number of consumer transactions outside China are currently conducted via credit or debit cards, inexorably replacing cash. The most recent trend toward a cashless society is enabled by *touchless Wi-Fi* and the nascent method of payment by cell phone.

Caveat: China has skipped a stage in payment technology. The use of credit cards and cash has already become marginal. More than 90 percent of the population in China's largest cities (nearly 50 percent in rural areas) use cell phones apps as their habitual payment method, through, for example, WeChat or Alipay. The speed of adoption of this payment method, unique in Asia, is because of it being consumer-friendly, convenient, fast, and accurate, and its universal incorporation of QR (Quick Response) codes, which were originally designed for the automotive industry in Japan. Even street performers use QR codes to collect contributions from the public. To conduct a transaction, a unique QR code, containing the user's banking details, is scanned either by the seller or the buyer.

Figure 6.1 QR LinkedIn logo

NB: scan the above QR code for further information.

Outcomes

The phenomenon of cell phone as a key buying tool is explained by the unaffordability of home computers for a large majority of the population, combined with the exponential growth of online trading. In 2018, over 80 percent of all payments in China were made by cell phone.

Case Study: Mitigating
Risk of Nonpayment

Expectations

Any company wanting to grow their exports, whatever products or services they offer, in whatever market segments, whatever scale of operation, price points, targeted territories, or commercial experience, they all need to trade with the lowest possible risk of nonpayment.

Unforeseen Dangers

As soon as goods or services are delivered to or collected by foreign customers, the supplier business is immediately exposed to the risk of not being paid (unless subject to payment in advance). Any business needs to make an informed assessment on how (or whether) to mitigate its exposure to default without incurring excessive costs.

Outcomes

Jean Roche, a French manufacturer of top-quality furniture, had trained their staff on international transactions. They systematically covered long-haul export orders with ICLC. This payment method, although costly and cumbersome, guarantees settlement, subject to detailed documentation being accurately completed. The surcharges that they applied to the product range to offset the cost of the ICLC did not affect the commerciality of the furniture in its premium marketplace.

An established outdoor clothing brand was large enough to have a highly proactive in-house customer credit control department. International insurance cover was used and in order to keep premiums at the lowest possible levels, close contact with the insurance groups, combined with an annual review of terms proved to be the best solution.

When insurance cover was not granted for whatever reason, but the customer was important for the company, appropriate research was conducted and based on the relationship and credit history with the customer, special payment options were individually negotiated to retain the business.

A French footwear manufacturer believed in buying commercial business data from a reliable source, for example, Dun & Bradstreet. This together with closely nurtured customer relationships limited their risks and obviated the need for credit insurance.

What actions should you take for your business?

Notes

_____

_____

_____

_____

_____

_____

CHAPTER 7

Culture and Behavior: Managing Organizational Disruption

"Never refuse an order"?

You have decided to export. As we have already addressed in preceding chapters, you may have taken this decision deliberately or opportunistically. You naturally have confidence that your current team can cope with the demands of your anticipated export business ... after all, they have helped you grow your company to its current size and success. In the past, they have overcome challenges as they have arisen, and although they may have little or no experience of exporting, you have every reason to believe that they are competent and will be hungry for this new treasure trove of opportunities.

In effect, your existing business is about to change beyond recognition. Managing and embracing this change to your systems, culture, and people, progressively and holistically, is the key to success. This process depends on your ability to develop or acquire a level of emotional intelligence across your teams that will allow them to listen actively and accurately to the marketplace. This in turn will enable them to reach effective decisions balancing consistent and sustainable export growth with the demands of the existing business.

Your teams will need to look beyond their current support resources and familiarize themselves with customs, duty, tariffs, packing lists, country of origin (CoO), bill of lading (BL), ATA (combination of French and English terms: admission temporaire or temporary admission) carnets, export health certificates (EHCs), pro-forma invoices, and so on. They are all strange new specialized processes, which have to become part of their daily routines. They may need to contact local embassies, chambers of commerce, revenue, and customs authorities to ensure watertight documentation compliance.

Entrenched thinking "we have always done it this way" and a lack of willingness to change in the face of your new export opportunities will limit your progress. Typically, fear of the unknown is at the root of resistance to change. Not grasping the real nature of the new challenges and knowing how to overcome them, combined with a natural inclination to keep things artificially simple, will inevitably hinder progress and strangle the opportunity at birth.

How will you approach successful exporting without the necessary skillsets?

(A)   Current Business

You have just received your first test export order. You have been actively looking for this for many months. It is disappointingly small compared to typical orders from your home market even after your sales team has committed a great deal of their time chasing it. You find that you need to devote considerably more time and effort to process this order and deliver it to the satisfaction of your new prospect. You have produced and allocated inventory for your new export customer to demonstrate your efficiency, but unexpectedly, a major existing client needs some of these lines. You decide to satisfy this customer to the detriment of the embryonic export account with an as yet unproved track record because there seems to be more at stake.

If you fail to pay the same attention to an export trial order as you would to your regular home market, your export business may never come to fruition. Even at this early stage in the relationship, the export customer may be forgiven for challenging you as to whether your products and service are really as good as you promised. Your customer will be expecting your delivered products to match your samples, and to sell through. They will want to be confident that you can replenish their inventory and deal swiftly with any complaints or returns. They will need you to communicate with them professionally and deliver according to their instructions. Ultimately, they will want to be sure that they can order again from you and in increasing quantities. The challenge here is to prioritize judiciously.

Have you addressed:

- your commitment to a dedicated export initiative?
- your alignment of the resources required for your home market with those needed to nurture your embryonic export business?
- how *fit for purpose* your current systems and processes are for exporting?
- the logistic requirements of your export accounts?
- how your teams will weigh up the demands of both markets?

How will you process your export orders without compromising your domestic business?

(B)   Production

After much stressful negotiation, you have finally received confirmation of an export order and agreed the product details and quantities, including any unavoidable customization, as well as delivery and payment terms. You expect that your current in-house production lines will cope. Where you have subcontractors to whom you are an important customer, you are confident that they will be prepared to accommodate your new demands.

Whether you have your own factories or you are sourcing through third parties in Eastern Europe, Asia, Africa, or any other region, you will need flexible and reliable capacity to draw on. This requires all parties to have the ability to speak your language, interpret your amended designs, and translate these into producing the specified items. Apart from the communication challenges, you may also need to review the capabilities of your machinery and the production licenses, which may be needed to comply with national regulations.

Your people will of course have to cope with new levels of pressure. In your own plants, as well as those of your suppliers, you will need to ensure that the technical abilities, skills, and qualifications of your staff and workforce are capable of servicing your anticipated export demands. The ages of their or your workers can be a significant obstacle to compliance with local authorities, particularly where children are employed.

Have you asked:

- how you will audit the working conditions and ages of your subcontractors' workforce?
- whether your subcontractors have the required certificates due to new product amends?
- how you will implement any required amendments to your products?
- what plant and machinery may have to be recalibrated to meet demands?
- what new machinery may be needed?
- what orders you may have to turn away if you or your suppliers cannot manufacture minimum or maximum quantities efficiently and economically?
- what disruption you may incur from abnormally large or … small orders?

How do product amendments impact your regular production?

(C)   Staff

You have taken the first steps to deal with a new export order. You believe that the enthusiasm of your staff, their excitement at this new direction, will lead them to handle the relevant procedures along the lines of your current home business. You are aware that some of them have basic foreign language skills, that some of them may be competent to research the documentation required to deliver the order, and you are satisfied that most of them understand and live the values of your business.

For your staff to feel valued and engaged to the point of delivering well beyond the minimum requirements for their job, you need to train, trust, and empower them. It is crucial to ensure that your teams are skilled and qualified enough to cover the new tasks presented by exporting, for example, they must be able to handle all the technical aspects of export business, such as certification, licenses, incoterms, payment methods, currency, choice of carrier, invoicing, value-added tax (VAT), as well as the ability to handle returns.

There is also the enormous challenge of communication and language. Your customer has every right to expect to be understood by your people at every stage of the transaction, as well as receive an appropriate, prompt, and clear response to any query. This will only be possible when you root out multicultural ignorance, which often leads to making precipitative judgments on unfamiliar behavior. To take full advantage of a variegated, innovative, fast-moving, and challenging market, you must develop and encourage a multicultural working environment. Equal attention needs to be paid to nurturing the attitude and aptitude for internationalization when developing your dedicated export team.

If your export strategy stretches you or your people beyond merely coping with random orders whenever they appear, you are now at the point of deciding to what extent you train or re-train your existing staff or recruit specialists on a full time or consultancy basis.

How will you assess:

- what new skills and competencies your organization requires?
- what international communication and language skills are needed?
- who has the appetite to learn the necessary new skills?
- what multicultural understanding is required, and how it is promoted internally?
- who will embrace the extra business potential with the appropriate attitude?
- who will grasp the bigger picture and vision for your business, and who may sabotage it unknowingly?
- who you will have to recruit internally and externally?
- who will own and lead your export initiative?

What budget have you allocated for re-training or recruiting permanent or consultancy staff?

(D)   Returns Policy

Your staff have an excellent service reputation in your home market. Your levels of returned goods are minimal. You are confident that your products or services are fit for purpose, will be delivered correctly, and paid for as expected. After all, you have effective control over the production processes, whether these are in-house or via third-party suppliers, and the logistics are proven. You believe that your current systems will be sufficient to deal with exports.

Irrespective of your history of successful performance locally, foreign customers may claim not to be completely satisfied when they receive their goods or services for a whole variety of new reasons. Whether you are trading online or via a subsidiary, the issue of returned products will arise and needs to be anticipated. This issue is exacerbated when you are exporting ... to the point of threatening your entire future in these markets.

Trading partners can be volatile in their buying intentions, and end-consumer brand loyalty is becoming ever more unpredictable. The proliferation of products and services as a result of globalization is so broad nowadays that people do not hesitate to switch from one item to another—even after having made their purchase, if they think that something else suits them better. Most major brands and retailers are now forced to accept returns, often without quibble, cost or recourse to the buyer, whatever the law of the land. This buying behavior has now become part of the expected service proposition in many countries. You, of course, will incur substantial extra handling costs, and your margins will be affected.

Thanks to the Internet, end-consumer behavior has progressed on a much greater scale from historical mail order buying habits to currently taking full advantage of the new online service levels offered. In the apparel and footwear markets, where online customers cannot try a product on before they buy it, they have become used to ordering several sizes and colors and sending back what they do not want, especially when there is little or no charge. There are cases where returns have reached up to 70 percent of deliveries in countries where products or services did not meet customer expectations.

Have you decided how to deal with:

- how and where you outline your returns policy?
- warranty claims now and in the future for business-to-business (B2B) or business-to-customer (B2C) transactions?

- the collection of goods to be returned?
- the assessment of genuine versus false claims? Who will inspect the returned goods?
- the repair or replacement and reshipping to the customer, reconditioning and reselling locally, repatriation, or destruction?
- the return of goods in units that have been exported in bulk, for example, documentation, transport, customs duties, VAT, and so on?
- how and when you reimburse customers who have sent goods back, which have been paid for? And, in what currency?
- the issuing of credit notes, a voucher for next purchase, or reimbursement of payment?
- the aggregate costs incurred by you and how you will recover them?

What is the potential cost of unanticipated returns?

(E)   Leadership

You have managed to deal successfully with your early export orders that your domestic sales team wrote and your admin and production teams processed and delivered. You hope that there are more to come, but there is no guarantee of future success. You want to keep your costs as low as possible and an open-ended investment in new infrastructure is out of the question ... anyway, when the next orders come in, you can grow on the profits they generate. *You'll manage.*

So, how serious are you about export?

If you do not know where you are heading, you are unlikely to arrive.

The stories of businesses with genuine potential that attempted to export without a clear vision, a focused strategy, and skilled people make for depressing reading. The lack of timely investment and a superficial understanding of the real issues, human and operational, combined with a *make-do* attitude may condemn an export initiative to early failure. Expecting inexperienced directors or unqualified managers, junior staff, or unskilled teams to deliver export success amounts to pure gambling . . . the odds are against you.

Experienced professional leadership is arguably the fundamental key to export success. Someone has to own the export project and lead the way. Ego or internal company politics must not be allowed to obstruct the assignment of this crucial responsibility to the right individual, whether he or she is from within your organization or a new recruit, a permanent appointment, or a consultant.

Enlightened leadership is vital at this point in your company's development. A business owner-manager, CEO, or MD has to promote and deliver an export initiative, which is totally integrated throughout every layer of the organization, not just an isolated department.

Have you decided:

- who will design your strategy, set objectives, and monitor progress?
- how much you are prepared to invest and where?
- which third-party funding, grants, export schemes, venture capital funds, so on are available?
- what skills and experience are essential for success?
- to promote staff from within or recruit?
- how you will establish your export priorities throughout your organization?
- how will you identify resistance to change, intentional or unintentional?
- who will lead?

What human resources do you need to lead your export journey?

Culture and Behavior: Managing Organizational Disruption—Key Learnings

1. Audit your suppliers' and customers' labor conditions and practices relentlessly. Be aware of slavery.

2. Evaluate when it is more profitable *not* to accept an order or advisable to sack a customer or client.

3. Ensure you have the production flexibility to cope with samples or nonstandard orders.

4. Make sure that you satisfy promising embryonic export customers without compromising existing domestic accounts.

5. Establish a detailed, cost-effective, and affordable returns policy from the outset.

6. Commit, lead, and train your entire organization in the adoption of an exporting mindset.

7. Do whatever it takes for your organization to embrace foreign languages and culture.

8. Encourage your teams to keep an open mind to any international opportunities and what they involve.

9. Create, embrace, and communicate a comprehensive export strategy incorporating short-, medium-, and long-term ambitions.

Case Study: E-Commerce in Germany

Expectations

Companies wishing to sell online in Europe may have taken the UK model on which to base their strategy. In 2017, the United Kingdom was well ahead of the other European countries in terms of value and volume online sales—circa 90 billion pounds (100 billion euros, 110 billion U.S. dollars) and growing rapidly.

Germany as the second largest e-market in Europe may understandably be targeted by exporters to expand their businesses.

Unforeseen Dangers

Uniquely, German buying habits, underpinned by local regulations, allowed consumers to return their unwanted purchases with very few restrictions. This resulted in an average of one in eight online orders being returned to suppliers. One in four customers sent back between 10 and 25 percent of all e-purchases. This was particularly prevalent in the clothing industry where style, color, size, fit, and texture are all key factors in satisfying the buyer. Return levels exceeding 25 percent were fairly common. And, the highest return levels originated from female and younger shoppers.

Outcomes

At such high levels of returns the management of these additional costs, unless passed on, can destroy an export initiative. There are known cases where companies have ceased to export to Germany online because of unsustainable levels of returns.

The impact of returns on suppliers has significant implications on logistics, personnel, processing, administration, and the ultimate resale or disposal of returned goods. The management of customer service expectations is equally complex, for example, time taken to send the goods back or have them collected and then be reimbursed.

Solutions adopted by companies to reduce these outcomes include the provision of: live chat online, forensic product information, 360-degree product imagery, videos, and so on. While these can be costly investments and will not entirely prevent returns, they may prove to be more cost effective than the basic approach to selling online in Germany.

Case Study: Clothing Manufacturers in Bangladesh

Expectations

Clothing brands worldwide recognized and used Bangladesh as a manufacturing base for their garment ranges at extremely competitive prices. Included in this list were prestige brands like Moncler, Prada, Versace, Gucci, as well as value-driven ranges for El Corte Ingles, Matalan, Primark, Bonmarché, Walmart, and so on. Bangladeshi manufacturers were viewed as long-term sustainable suppliers to Western markets, allowing their customers to enjoy generous margins.

Unforeseen Dangers

Working practices and conditions in Bangladesh had been under scrutiny since the Spectrum factory collapse in 2005. This had led to the creation of the ethical trading initiative (ETI) and the business social compliance initiative (BSCI) by major textile brands in an attempt to collaborate on minimum working conditions.

Nonetheless, in 2013 an eight-story building, Savar, which housed five clothing factories employing over 5,000 workers, along with other businesses and apartments, collapsed with the loss of 1,134 lives. A further 2,500 workers and residents had to be rescued. This was viewed as the deadliest structural failure in recent times.

The original building did not anticipate accommodating over 5,000 workers. Four additional floors had been added, ignoring building regulations. The structure was never intended to support the weight and operation of heavy machinery.

Many well-known brands were manufactured within these premises.

Outcomes

The media worldwide picked up the story and investigated it. It reported that tight manufacturing deadlines and demand for the lowest cost production methods had led to minimal supervision by local managers. There were no trade unions in Bangladesh to protect workers, as this would have added costs and reduced the appeal of their *competitive* garment manufacturing industry. Many brands were named and shamed by the media, potentially affecting their image adversely.

In an attempt to repair their reputation and cope with similar situations in the future, most of the brands established direct factory assessment procedures under their own individual control requiring certification. Furthermore, major retailers started to demand ETI certification from the brands to be distributed in their stores.

What actions should you take for your business?

Notes

_____

_____

_____

_____

_____

_____

The Way Forward: Driving Success

If you have read this far, you will now have most of the tools to move forward and develop an export business to the level to which you aspire. You need to be clear in your definition and measurement of success. The lists of key learnings from each chapter reveal *three* essential considerations for generating that success—*attitude, research,* and *strategy.*

Attitude: Keep it simple at the beginning. You should leverage the products and services that you already offer wherever possible and bring your current teams in to line with your enthusiasm for export. However, exporting should be regarded as more than a quick fix to boost sales. The most successful exporters are patient and proactive; they are prepared to initiate and foster relationships with overseas buyers and consumers over the long term. They are constantly looking for rewarding opportunities and sustainable partnerships. Determination over time and in the face of unforeseen events will ensure that your export initiatives are successful.

Above all, you must have an open mind to whatever your research tells you and be prepared to replace any preconceptions with respect for your consumers in every way. Humility is an asset.

Extensive *research* into the habits and behaviors of consumers in your target markets, whether B2B or direct-to-customer (D2C), is paramount and ongoing. It will always pay dividends if you embrace and answer their genuine needs. Today, market intelligence gathering can be conducted online at any time. To supplement and verify your findings, go and see for yourself. Visit your chosen territory. Attend appropriate tradeshows and events for real-time networking and learning.

Strategy: The adoption of a well-thought-out and realistic business plan is the foundation on which you build your export venture. This is the blueprint for your commercial future, and any ensuing actions should relate to it. It is a living document and will inevitably need to be amended, extended, and updated according to changing conditions. It is the structure underpinning the vision that you and your staff are committed to deliver.

End game: Wherever in the world you are, there will typically be many helpful resources at your disposal. Government agencies will offer extensive grants and guidance. You may typically contact your national or local chamber of commerce or board of trade. Your government department responsible for encouraging export may appear to be a cost-effective first resort. A more relevant resource may be provided by your local or international trade or professional association.

Expectations toward these bodies are often unrealistic. Your ambitions are more likely to be met if you have first developed a clear strategy regarding what territories you are targeting with what products or services and in what timeframe. The more specific you can be, the more likely you are to receive constructive advice.

The organization that focuses on creating a comprehensive strategy using a dedicated in-house team and recruiting qualified professionals will, in our experience, succeed more rapidly and sustainably.

About the Authors

Laurent Houlier has over 27 years' experience in successfully delivering holistic international strategies and leadership for a variety of European fast-moving consumer goods (FMCG) organizations.

He has taken domestic companies and pioneered their brands all over the world. His specialty is in selecting the most suitable channel mix, designing strategies to maximize their performance in the most sustainable way.

He was integral in winning the Queen's Award for International Trade over several years for a major UK brand.

He attended Audencia Business School (France). Laurent graduated in management, finance, and accounting, specializing in marketing and international trade. Laurent has a passion for foreign cultures and introduces himself as *Citizen of the World*. He is conversant in Russian and Mandarin Chinese, has a working knowledge of Dutch and Italian, and is fluent in French, English, German, and Spanish.

John Blaskey has over 45 years of practical commercial experience. He has generated hundreds of millions of pounds of new prospective business across the world for his clients via his company The Exhibiting Agency Ltd.

John addresses how to identify and recruit real business prospects, how to evaluate them, how to listen actively to their stated needs, how to align their messaging consistently, and how to take full advantage of international face-to-face marketing.

He has developed proven tools and processes that are delivered via workshops, masterclasses, keynotes, consultancy, and books. His approach deliberately disrupts conventional presentation norms.

John's clients include

Government trade organizations: China, Dubai, Hong Kong, Indonesia, Italy, Kenya, Korea, Latvia, Thailand.

Global multinationals: Agfa, Alere, AstraZeneca, British Standards Institute, EDF, Fuji Film Sericol, GE Finance, Howden Engineering, Instron, La-z-Boy, Mitsubishi, OKI, Terumo, Triumph Lingerie, Vanguard Industries (Oman).

Trade associations: Association of Event Organizers, British Promotional Merchandise Association, Council of Mortgage Lenders, Farnborough Airshow, IPSE (association for Independent Professionals and the Self-Employed (UK)), Made in Vicenza, Marketing Manchester, Meetings Industry Association, Royal Aeronautical Society, Society of Motor Manufacturers and Traders, UFI (Union des Foires Internationales), UKTI (United Kingdom Trade and Investment).

. . . and hundreds of small and medium enterprises (SMEs), too numerous to mention.

Index

www.ingramcontent.com/pod-product-compliance
Lightning Source LLC
Chambersburg PA
CBHW061329220326
41599CB00026B/5104